Praise for *The Membership Economy*

"Having seen and experienced the challenges of building long-term sustainable relationships involving membership organizations, Robbie Kellman Baxter offers clear examples and straightforward advice how to achieve success in both the non-profit and corporate sectors."

> Howard L. Wollner, Chairman, NPR Foundation

"There's a big difference between subscribers and members. From The Times to The Sun and now at the Wall Street Journal, we are committed to building our relationship with our customers around the principles of membership. Members are more engaged, more connected and more profitable. Read *The Membership Economy* to learn how to take your organisation from transactional to relational."

> Katie Vanneck-Smith, Chief Customer Officer and
> Global Managing Director, Dow Jones

"As the leader of a major alumni relations office, I understand the importance of building long term relationships with our members. Robbie Kellman Baxter's practical advice will drive immediate results. If your organization depends on having highly engaged members, you should read *The Membership Economy*."

> Raphe Beck, Director of Alumni Relations, Stanford
> Graduate School of Business

"I've run a successful membership business for a while now. So I'd like to tell you to move along and not read this book... because why is Robbie Kellman Baxter giving away all our hard-won secrets...? But I won't tell you that. Because *The Membership Economy* is great perspective on an important topic."

> Ann Handley, Chief Content Officer of MarketingProfs,
> and author of the WSJ bestseller, *Everybody Writes*

"Robbie's book is packed with innovative ideas for pricing, acquisition and engagement of customer. I highly recommend this book for any CEO who seeks to disrupt their industry by putting their customers at the center of everything they do."

> Heidi Roizen, Operating Partner, Draper, Fisher, Jurvetson

"From Netflix to Spotify, over the past few years, subscription models have become a powerful and profitable business model in the digital economy. Robbie has written a unique, well-researched and very smart book for anyone interested in building one."

> David Kirchhoff, former CEO, Weight Watchers
> International and WeightWatchers.com

...MBERSHIP ECONOMY

Find Your Superusers, Master the Forever Transaction, and Build Recurring Revenue

ROBBIE KELLMAN BAXTER

New York   Chicago   San Francisco   Athens   London
Madrid   Mexico City   Milan   New Delhi
Singapore   Sydney   Toronto

3 4 5 6 7 8 9 0 DOC/DOC 1 2 0 9 8 7 6 5

ISBN: 978-0-07-183932-7
MHID: 0-07-183932-1

e-ISBN: 978-0-07-183933-4
e-MHID: 0-07-183933-X

Library of Congress Cataloging-in-Publication Data

Baxter, Robbie Kellman.
 The membership economy : find your super users, master the forever transaction, and build recurring revenue / Robbie Kellman Baxter.
     pages cm
   ISBN 978-0-07-183932-7 (alk. paper) — ISBN 0-07-183932-1 (alk. paper)
 1. Customer clubs. 2. Marketing. 3. Customer relations. I. Title.
   HF5415.525.B39 2015
   658.8'7—dc23

                                                                2015001215

McGraw-Hill Education books are available at special quantity discounts to use as premiums and sales promotions, or for use in corporate training programs. To contact a representative, please visit the Contact Us page at www.mhprofessional.com.

For my parents, who think I'm great no matter what.

CONTENTS

SECTION III Membership Organizations Come in All Shapes and Sizes

FOREWORD

Belonging matters. Each of us yearns for the tribe: for the affiliations that will support us, protect us, define us, help us make sense of a complex and overwhelming world. Everyday conversation revolves as much as ever around belonging: Do you use an iPhone or Android? Are you a Millennial—or not? The one percent or the ninety-nine?

Belonging is powerful, so powerful it's dangerous. It includes us, but makes us insular. It informs us, but makes us ignorant of other views. It makes a big world feel small and comfortable, for better *and* worse. Underlying Robbie Baxter's book is a theme we have discovered at LinkedIn: Memberships only work when based on mutual respect and benefit. She talks about Gainsight, which reconceives Customer Service into Customer Success; Amazon and their focus on value; mileage programs that fail when they stop valuing the members. When you treat your customers like members, you invest in them. It's the only way they will invest in you.

But understanding belonging and how to build it is only one reason you need this book. The second? This book describes the future.

Robbie isn't writing about tech companies *per se*; but the companies she writes about have embraced the opportunities and changes technology has brought in the last fifteen years. Those changes include two-way conversations with large member bases, big data to understand customer success and your business instantaneously, cloud computing, full personalization of customer service, and much more—in short, changes which allow any business to become a membership business.

When Robbie reached out to me a few months ago to talk about the book she was writing on the Membership Economy, I wasn't sure we needed this book. Surely, most folks at this point have an understanding of membership, right? We've all experienced it: felt that feeling of privilege and belonging or felt betrayed when the relationship with our club or brand broke down.

But when Robbie sent me the manuscript for the book, it took me about two chapters to realize that I was wrong. The minute I got to Maslow and the importance of belonging, I knew she was about to broaden my perspective on what has always been one of the central, evolving themes in LinkedIn's product and business.

Business itself is changing. Software as a service, the sharing economy, digitization of physical goods, and the arrival of virtual goods—these trends represent only the beginning of the coming change. As the cost of physical goods drops due to automation, as the world of manufacturing becomes massively distributable through 3D printing and other cheap manufacturing technologies, as just-in-time logistics become a commodity, the whole idea of owning things is going to change.

And that's where Robbie begins her discussion: the swinging of the pendulum between Membership and Ownership. It's on its way to Membership. And this time, it might end up staying there.

So enjoy her insights, and consider her eminently applicable strategies and tactics.

Your membership in the Membership Economy is waiting. Your free trial starts now.

Allen Blue
Cofounder, LinkedIn
Venice, California,
September 2014

ACKNOWLEDGMENTS

Writing this book is one of the most challenging, creative, frustrating, and rewarding things I have ever done. Writing a book is mostly a lonely, singular path. As an extrovert, it's hard for me to work that way. So I reached out to many, many people for help. Amazingly, nearly all the people I asked were generous in sharing their time and expertise. Even the professionals who were officially being paid to help me went over and above what I ever would have expected. Without my colleagues, friends, and family, I never would have finished. I need to extend my deepest gratitude to many people:

To the pioneers of the Membership Economy who allowed me to include their stories and words and who connected me with others: Jim Adkins, John Baker, Kerry Barlas, Iniko Basilio, Bob Baxley, Jamie Beckland, Dave Beckwith, Alex Benn, Allen Blue, Bruce Clarke, Miranda Coykendall, Elizabeth Crosta, Kevin Donnellan, Michelle Epstein, Michael Geller, John Graham, Reggie Henry, Gene Hoffman, David Hyman, Brian Jacobs, Vineet Jain, Arthur Johnson, Matt Johnson, Ajay Kaushal, Clark Kepler, David Kirchhoff, Tom Krackeler, John Kremer, Becca Krass, Jimi Letchford, Praveen Madan, Fran Maier, Tim Maly, Lisa Mann, Tim McDonald, Chris McGill, Nick Mehta, Cathi Nelson, Guy Nirpaz, Lindsay Pedersen, Rajesh Ram, Nancy Redd, Joff Redfern, Tanya Roberts, Cary Rozenzweig, Garret Seevers, Leyla Seka, Paul Shoemaker, Josh Silverman, Anne Marie Squeo, Mollie Starr, Dawn Sweeney, Tien Tzuo, Camille Watson, Tim Westergren, and Michael Wu and to all my clients who allowed me to test new ideas and be a part of their journeys, and who have been a source of inspiration.

To my early reviewers: I am lucky to have friends who can write and edit and give me feedback in a way that I can hear it and use it. To my incredibly talented friends and colleagues who spent hours and hours reading and editing my drafts, combining tough love with encouragement when I needed it most: Rebecca Bloom, Oona Ceder, Liza Hanks, Seth Kahan, Camille Landau, Cindy Lee, Laura Lowell, Linda Popky, and Becca Britton Pecore, for reading many chapters and sections quickly and carefully, and for making the book much better.

I won the friendship trifecta with Joanna Strober, who is a best-selling author, Membership Economy entrepreneur, and a source of daily support and wisdom. To my girlfriends who have been there for me through this long journey, with patience and kindness, even when I didn't return their calls: Julie Andersson, Roxanne Bozdog, Lauren Calhoon, Maile Creamer, Jeanne Lowell, Laura Missan, Jessica Olson, Parke Treadway, and Jill Zanolli, all of whom reached out to me when I was in my tunnel and saw the light at the end even when I didn't.

To my consulting colleagues and especially the following: Scott Edinger, Seth Kahan, Lisa McLeod, Linda Popky, Libby Wagner, and Scott Wintrip, who encouraged me to think big.

To my consulting mentor, Alan Weiss, who has taught me so much about so many things, and who first got me thinking seriously about writing a business book. And to all the many people in Alan's community who have become friends and colleagues over the years—so many of you have offered introductions, writing tips, and encouragement along the way.

To my friends who have written books and who answered my never-ending questions about everything from agents and proposals, to editing and promoting the book itself: Leslie Crutchfield, Denise Brousseau, Dorie Clark, Heather McLeod Grant, Bill Lee, Charlene Li, Liz Lynch, Roberta Matuson, Sharon Meers, Adrian Ott, Amanda Setili, Andrew Sobel, Lisa Solomon, and all of the women from the Authoress circle.

To the publishing and writing professionals who challenged, guided, and helped me get this book written and published: my writing coach Mark Levy, who helped me find my voice and sparked my creativity;

Sarah White, who helped me restructure the whole book over a long, intense Independence Day weekend and then polished with me right up to the deadline; Wally Wood, who hammered all of my writing chunks into a single smooth story; my agent, Ted Weinstein, who pushed me to make my proposal tight, clear, and compelling and helped me sign with McGraw-Hill; and Donya Dickerson and the McGraw-Hill team, including Scott Kurtz, Cheryl Hudson, Roberta Mantus, Ann Pryor, Robert Swanson, and Chelsea Van Der Gaag, who saw the promise of the Membership Economy, took my words, made them into a real book and brought that book out into the world.

Most of all, I want to express gratitude to my family. To my children who have heard enough about the Membership Economy to write a book of their own about it; to my sister who is such a fine writer herself and inspired me to be more candid, authentic, and helpful, through her example; to all the Baxters and Agustins who were always in my corner; to my mom and dad who read the book several times and offered detailed feedback and unabashed encouragement and support.

And to Bob, who lets me wake him to share my worries, who has read and edited just about every word I've written since we were sophomores in college, and who is still my very best friend and advisor after all this time.

Introduction

I started writing this book, at least in my mind, about 10 years ago. I live in Silicon Valley and have been here for most of my life. For the past 13 years, I have been running a strategy consulting firm, and early on, most of my clients were Silicon Valley technology companies.

About 10 years, ago, I started working with Netflix. You're probably familiar with that company. It's the guys who created House of Cards and Orange Is the New Black, two of my favorite shows. But back then, they were known for being the online DVD rental subscription company. It took a lot of words to describe them, because their model was unlike anything out there.

Netflix used technology to dramatically improve the experience of renting movie DVDs. By the time I started consulting for them, I was already a loyal subscriber. I loved being able to build a queue of movies I was interested in, so I always had three waiting for me, loved being able to order from home and have them delivered, and most of all, I loved the fact that there were no late fees. Ever. I was an evangelist. I loved them.

But I loved them even more as a consultant. I thought that Netflix was the most exciting company I had ever worked with. Its model was smart and simple. Unlimited DVDs, three out at a time, for a fixed price. Subscribers sign up once, but become loyal subscribers forever—or at least for several years.

Unlike the rental stores that depended on each transaction to drive revenue, Netflix started out in the early days with just one "forever transaction"—after you sign up and until you cancel, you get the same great experience without having to enter your payment information ever again.

1

For the subscriber, it meant constant movies and low stress. For Netflix, it meant recurring revenue. And the experience was so good it created a whole subset of superusers, the loyal product evangelists who educated the market about the Netflix service, while providing helpful feedback to the company.

The Netflix model was disruptive. There were very few digital subscription businesses of any real size at that time. Netflix didn't have a lot to compare itself to, besides HBO and maybe the cell phone companies. But it was onto something—and it was all about membership, not ownership. I was hooked on the model and went on to advise dozens of companies on their subscription and community businesses. It was so obvious to me that technology was enabling new ways of engaging customers in an ongoing, authentic way, and I saw potential everywhere. Others saw it too. One VC told me, "Membership is the holy grail." It has so many advantages.

I'm convinced that the Membership Economy will have as profound an effect on society as the Industrial Revolution or the spread of the automobile. And the leaders who ignore it will follow carriage makers into oblivion. And yet I'm surprised by how many people haven't seen this transformation. That's why I'm writing this book.

What Is the Membership Economy?

So what is the Membership Economy? Some say it's all about subscriptions. Others say it's about community and communication. Still others say it's about belonging. Some say it's been around forever, in associations, loyalty programs, and gyms.

I think the Membership Economy is all these things. I define membership as the state of being formally engaged with an organization or group on an ongoing basis. Members are part of the whole—although they don't always contribute to the experience of other members. An organization able to build relationships with *members*—as opposed to plain *customers*—has, as we'll see, a powerful competitive edge. It's not just changing the words you use; it's about changing the way you think about the people you serve and how you treat them.

The Membership Economy model works for both organizations and individuals. Executives and investors alike see that the model succeeds because it reduces uncertainty in their revenue. When done correctly, membership appeals to the members too, because membership provides recognition, stability, and convenience while connecting people to one another.

Today, the promise of membership is greater than ever. Evolving technologies have dramatically enhanced the ability of a broad range of industries to take advantage of membership models. The Membership Economy is all about putting the customer at the center of the business model rather than the product or the transaction. Every organization should be focused on the customer. The business model and organization need to support this customer-centric model. The relationship between customer and organization is ongoing and formal, a "forever transaction" that has implications across the organization, changing everything.

The Membership Economy brings together my two loves, business and psychology. It gets its power from connecting to deep human needs. According to psychologist Abraham Maslow, after satisfying physiological needs and safety, people focus on needs of belonging and esteem before ultimately moving to self-actualization. The Membership Economy helps people satisfy those needs.

I Wrote This Book for You

This book contains strategies for the Membership Economy that can be used by nearly any type of organization, as well as examples of some of the many kinds of organizations that are already leveraging the power of membership and guidelines to help you navigate key moments of transformation.

Hopefully the book will help you think more broadly about what's possible and provide guidance for what to do next. Readers who will benefit most from the book include:

- *Executives* in product-centric companies seeking to join the Membership Economy.

- *Entrepreneurs* building new organizations who want to incorporate the power of membership from the outset.
- *Association leaders* who worry about declining membership satisfaction.
- *Marketers* who run "loyalty programs" that have become commoditized.
- *Board members* looking for new models to strengthen their companies, build stronger customer relationships, and drive more predictable revenue streams.
- *Community organizers* who want to bring people together.
- *Business school students* who will be influencing tomorrow's business models.
- *Individuals* who care about connection and belonging.

How to Read This Book

I have written this book with the understanding that time-pressed readers browse and dive into books as their interests dictate. You will find four sections, each with several chapters:

- **Section I:** What You Need to Know About the Membership Economy
- **Section II:** Membership Economy Strategies and Tactics
- **Section III:** Membership Economy Organizations Come in All Shapes and Sizes
- **Section IV:** The Membership Economy and Transformation: Key Inflection Points

You can read the book from start to finish—the ideas build on each other. But feel free to jump around—reading only what seems most relevant or interesting to you. You will find terms defined in the glossary at the end of the book.

It is my deepest wish that this book is inspiring and helpful to everyone who picks it up and that it enables greater connection and meaning in your business, civic, and personal spheres.

While I hope you find the book entertaining and fun to read, I *really* hope you apply some of the tips and techniques to build a business that is less lumpy, more predictable, more valuable to your members, and ultimately more profitable for you.

—Robbie Kellman Baxter
Menlo Park, California

SECTION I WHAT YOU NEED TO KNOW ABOUT THE MEMBERSHIP ECONOMY

Before you invest any time in learning about the Membership Economy and how to apply its principles, you probably want to know what it is, why it's important, and how it can help you. If the transactional model is dying and the Membership Economy is replacing it, what does that mean?

This first section provides an overview of how the Membership Economy fits into the bigger picture, why it matters, and what it looks like.

Membership is a concept that is timeless, important, and powerful. It is part of our innate humanity to gravitate toward community. Once trade economies developed, we proved we were willing to pay a premium for connection, and the Membership Economy was born.

In Chapter 1 you will learn how the Membership Economy fits into the pattern common to most transformative business trends and how subscription—a model we've long been accustomed to—both resembles and differs from the Membership Economy model. Likewise the sharing economy is introduced and compared to the Membership Economy.

In Chapter 2 we delve deeper into the cultural transformation that is underway that is shifting us from an economy based on principles of ownership to one based on access. This swing explains the current interest in and success of Membership Economy business models.

In Chapter 3 we introduce you to six overarching categories of Membership Economy organizational models, categories that I use throughout the book to help you identify your place in the Membership Economy both as a consumer (member) and as a business leader responsible for your organization's strategy.

The three chapters in Section I will help you get the big picture and set the stage for the next sections, which get into specific strategies, tactics, and situations.

1

How the Membership Economy Fits into the Bigger Picture

We hear the stories. Cornered by a passionate friend, we are regaled with stories of a binge-watching House of Cards, or the virtues of the Paleo diet combined with Crossfit, or the new songs discovered by Pandora. A certain type of organization is winning the hearts and voices of their customers, and building the kind of loyalty that traditionally was reserved for family, community, and church. The secret that these organizations know is that people are craving membership. Organizations that build their businesses around people's needs to belong, to be connected, and to be admired, that are focused on relationships over products, are winning in today's economy.

You probably picked up this book because you want to understand how these organizations are building such loyalty, and how many of them have built recurring revenue models, the "holy grail" of business. The good news is that it's possible for just about any type of organization to incorporate principles of membership into their businesses. The Membership Economy is transforming the way organizations connect with their customers, and this book will tell you how.

To understand why the Membership Economy is becoming so vibrant and how it fits into the bigger picture, we have to take a step back. As a society, we are moving faster and spending less time in traditional communities. This alienation is driving consumers to seek greater flexibility and connection, often from new kinds of organizations, going beyond the traditional clubs, churches, and family gatherings of the past.

In *Bowling Alone: The Collapse and Revival of American Community*,[1] published in 2001, Robert Putnam shows how we have become increasingly disconnected from family, friends, neighbors, and our democratic structures—and how we may reconnect with them. Putnam draws on evidence including nearly 500,000 interviews conducted over a quarter of a century to demonstrate that we sign fewer petitions, belong to fewer organizations that hold meetings, know our neighbors less well, meet with friends less frequently, and even socialize with our families less often than in the past. To use Putnam's bowling metaphor, more of us are bowling more than ever before, but we're not bowling in leagues. We're bowling alone.

> Membership is timeless, important, and powerful.

The Membership Economy is a reaction to the social trend Putnam identified. The Membership Economy is enabling all kinds of organizations to build social capital and create meaningful connections. Maybe it's not that we're no longer connected, but rather that our connections are popping up in new places, many of which are enabled by new technologies.

A shift has begun. Membership is timeless, important, and powerful. People crave it. My town has a neighborhood of closely packed houses, designed to look like "small town America." The development forbids tall front yard fences and gates, sidewalks abound, and there's even a small "neighborhood" park. A few blocks away, in an equally convenient and prestigious area, is a second neighborhood with bigger yards and bigger houses, but people pay the same amount as they do for the privilege of living in the smaller houses in the stronger community.

In other words, people seem to be willing to pay a premium for connection, for a neighborhood. They are willing to give up privacy in exchange for association with others. A membership organization builds a "neighborhood" for its ideal customer. There's a cost associated both with buying and maintaining a house in a neighborhood, so the promise of connection, community, and ongoing value must be guaranteed.

The Difference Between Membership and Subscription

Membership is an attitude, an emotion. A *subscription* is a financial arrangement. It's quite possible for something to be both a subscription *and* a membership organization. In fact, the Membership Economy is the logical extension of subscriptions. Many Membership Economy organizations don't see themselves as membership. They say, "We have a subscription business," or "We're a sharing business," or "We're a transactional company with an affinity program," or "We're a social network." Sometimes they say that membership organizations must be mission-driven nonprofits or about connections among members.

None of this is true.

What makes a membership organization is the attitude of the organization and the feelings of its members—not whether members subscribe. Companies' failure to see themselves as part of this bigger trend can limit their potential to build relationships and strengthen their models.

A subscription does give access and an array of choices. A transactional customer might own dozens or even hundreds of movies. But Netflix has thousands—from different countries, genres, and more— providing tremendous choice and the latest options. And the monthly price is low which protects the customer's cash flow. Access is so much bigger than ownership, and the subscription model ties customers to organizations in an ongoing relationship with an opportunity for benefits on both sides.

Those are simple subscription benefits. But some of the value subscribers get from Netflix is derived from the other people using it and their comments about movies and TV shows. This value comes from the community. Netflix also created an algorithm that harvests the data it collects in order to analyze its members' behavior. It can use the information it gets to provide recommendations for other films.

Even with all these benefits, many Netflix subscribers may not feel like members, and that's okay because they're still part of the Membership Economy. Even without using the nomenclature of membership and even without investing in the community side, both the company and the customers are benefiting from the application of the principles of the Membership Economy.

What Brought Us to This Point?

The shift to a Membership Economy follows a pattern that is common to many transformative business trends. It's brought on by an outside force, ties into a human need, and impacts a wide range of industries and companies. Eventually, the trend becomes part of the new normal, is taught in business schools and is practiced by managers. Let's take a look at each of these:

1. *The shift is brought on as a result of a major outside force.*
    There are actually two major outside forces combining to drive the Membership Economy: The ubiquity of online access via multiple devices, which connect members with content, services, other members, and the company itself at all times, and the dramatically declining costs of data storage and processing, which enable companies to store and provide access to services at a very low price.

    The first phase of online access was a one-way connection in which the organization was able to provide services and content to customers. More recently, however, technology has grown more sophisticated, thus allowing individuals to respond to the organizations, providing feedback and new content while also enabling peer connection among customers.

For example, General Motors recently used its Facebook page to respond to concerns and questions relating to its recall of 1.6 million cars that had been linked to a dozen deaths.[2] Technology enables the transformation from users to members and creates community and interdependence among the users themselves.

At the same time, costs of data processing and storage as well as Internet connectivity costs have been declining, making it easier for organizations to bear these costs on behalf of their customers, and enabling them to think about pricing in a more sophisticated way.

Ubiquitous and inexpensive access has created the ideal conditions for the Membership Economy.

2. *It ties into a timeless human need.*

Pundits never get tired of lamenting the decline of face-to-face community and belonging that has been brought about by the advances of the Internet. Yet technology enables us to be connected in ways never before possible. I Skype with clients in South Africa, Greece, and Asia, and I can instantly poll hundreds of other consultants for advice through my online professional network. Without boarding a plane or even changing out of my pajama bottoms, I can strengthen my social network virtually any time I have a few minutes.

> We're not limited today by physical proximity in our associations.

Humans yearn to be connected and to gain energy, knowledge, and comfort from others. The communities that are most meaningful and impactful may not be the same as those in the past—neighborhood mothers, religious organizations, and professional associations—but people are still finding ways to stay connected. We're not limited today by physical proximity in our associations.

Facebook, for all the complaints about people posting their mundane breakfasts and breakups, has been instrumental in bringing together families, reconnecting old friends, and even saving lives. In the summer of 2014, the ALS Ice Bucket Challenge, a fundraising campaign to raise money by having individuals challenge their friends to dump a bucket of ice water on their heads or pay $100 to the ALS Foundation, was the hit of the summer, clogging our Instagram feeds and quadrupling the donations from the prior year.[3]

Through membership, members can be perceived as important, connected, or successful. In short, membership makes us feel good.

3. *The impact can be seen across a wide range of industries and companies.* Examples of how the Membership Economy is transforming industries and companies are limitless. A hair salon in California sells subscription haircuts and encourages socializing at the salon. Organizations like news sites DIGG, Reddit, and News360 are transforming how consumers receive, evaluate, and prioritize news content. YouTube lets us all be stars for professional advancement and personal satisfaction. Photo sharing sites like Flickr, Pinterest, and Snapfish allow photo enthusiasts to connect with one another, and the Association of Personal Photo Organizers (APPO) trains and connects the professionals who assist photo enthusiasts with their images.

Once you start thinking about how the principles of membership can be incorporated into existing business models, you start to see opportunities everywhere. The implication is clear: this model is likely relevant to you.

4. *Eventually, this trend becomes part of the new normal.* Business schools now teach subscription marketing, and nearly every major company has a team dedicated to building community and belonging around even the most mundane products. Organizations are investing in ongoing relationship-building and customer success, going well beyond traditional tech support cost centers of the past.

The Membership Economy brings together business and psychology because the membership economy gets its energy from deep human needs.

The Membership Economy helps people satisfy those needs—on an ongoing basis—since most membership businesses leverage some kind of ongoing subscription. However, there is a considerable difference between a membership-based and a subscription-based organization.

The Difference Between Membership and Sharing

Because of my expertise in the Membership Economy, I am often asked to comment on other "new economies." One of those, the *sharing economy*, is closely related to the Membership Economy.

> *Many of the most successful sharing economy businesses depend on the Membership Economy.*

The sharing economy is a model based on sharing (or renting) assets not currently being used—a car, a spare bedroom, a vacation home. While there is a lot of interest in the sharing economy right now, the idea itself is not new. "Sharing economy" is a relatively new term and is very trendy. But you can point to older instances—vacation rentals by owner (VRBO), for example. They're based on the principle that there is stored value in expensive assets and by making them available to others when we don't use them, we can unlock that value. It's a sustainable economic system built around peer-to-peer sharing of underutilized assets. Examples include Airbnb, RelayRides, and Napster.

Many of the most successful sharing economy businesses depend on the Membership Economy. A feeling of membership infrastructure is needed so that people can extend trust beyond the people in their physical communities. In my view the sharing economy is a subset of the Membership Economy.

When people talk about the sharing economy, they're talking about people sharing stuff that belongs to other individuals and not to an organization. For example, consider RelayRides. You might come to San Francisco where I live and need to rent a car. Meanwhile, my car is just sitting in the driveway most of the time because I can walk to work. You can rent my car for less than the cost of a traditional rental.

In contrast, Netflix has a membership business where consumers share access to a wide selection of content, but the content belongs to the company and not the individuals. It's not me sharing with you—it's Netflix providing access to its content to all of us.

Changes in technology have enabled sharing to take off. What enables a large-scale sharing business is trust. The Internet makes it possible to build trusted systems. Always-on mobile devices that enable us to connect at any time make it more efficient to share. Ten years ago if you and I had wanted to share a car and didn't know each other, it would have been hard to impossible to broker that situation. But with today's technology—big data evaluating in real time your trustworthiness and mine as well as locating my car—it is relatively easy to identify my unused asset and your unmet need.

Sharing makes the most sense in areas where the assets are expensive, varied, and underutilized. Vacation homes, cars, collections of content, and special-occasion clothing are all assets that are generally underutilized and are, not surprisingly, some of the early successes of the sharing economy.

Remember

The Membership Economy has come about and is growing because of massive social trends and developing technology. The computer and the Internet are changing human lives in ways as profound as the mass production of the automobile, which changed everything from the way we courted to the way we shopped. In the midst of this change, however, human needs remain constant. How to shape an enterprise that meets those needs is the subject of the chapters just ahead.

2 | Why the Membership Economy Matters

Try this. Google "membership." The majority of your results will be museums, churches, and other nonprofits. The term *membership* is owned by nonprofits and a few loyalty clubs—but that's it. And that's a shame, because, as I show, the Membership Economy contains many more organization types than nonprofits and loyalty programs. Indeed, when an organization is structured around the customer, with an ongoing and formal relationship between customer and organization, it becomes a membership company almost by default.

From Ownership to Access

In the past, much of our economy has operated on the principles of ownership. Companies sell things, and consumers *buy* them and *own* them. The idea of ownership is simple—if it's mine, it's mine. I can alter, destroy, sell, or save my stuff, and I can use it for as long as I'd like. However, it also means that I have the responsibilities that come with ownership.

Many of us own cars, and there are certainly benefits to ownership. If you want to paint flames on the side of your car or lift or lower the chassis or customize your plates, you have to own the car. But if your car breaks down or a fender-bender takes out a headlight, you need to fix it. If it becomes expensive to maintain, you need to decide whether to invest in a new model or live with, and be seen in, unreliable wheels.

> *Ownership and access are at two ends of a continuum, and right now the pendulum is swinging away from owning.*

If you need to use the car only occasionally, don't have a garage, or want to always drive the latest model, ownership may not be your best choice. Other options exist if you want access to a car. You can rent one, lease one, or call a cab. But none of these options has truly taken advantage of the Membership Economy.

Today, technology has provided new models for drivers that were unavailable in the past. These include Zipcar, which provides members access to a fleet of company-owned cars for single-trip usage without requiring "by-the-day" rental; RelayRides, which allows members to rent the cars of other members when the cars are not in use; and Uber, a car service which allows anyone with a luxury car to become a driver for hire.

Ownership and access are at two ends of a continuum, and right now the pendulum is swinging away from owning. As individuals grow frustrated with the burdens of owning, caring for, and storing too much stuff, they are looking for ways to minimize that stress. They are also experiencing a need for meaningful connection and community. The Membership Economy provides a solution to both of these challenges: simultaneously minimizing the burdens of ownership while offering new ways to derive a sense of community.

Table 2.1 charts the key differences between ownership and the Membership Economy.

The key metrics in the ownership economy are conversion rate, transaction size, and economies of scale. In the Membership Economy they are retention and customer lifetime value.

	Ownership Economy	Membership Economy
Key Metrics	Conversion, transaction size, manufacturing economies of scale	Lifetime customer value/ retention
Customer Value Path	Cross-sell	Tiers of value and add-ons
Personalization	Customization	Configuration
Sampling	Free sample or trial	Free trial and freemium
Key Organizational Objective	Control	Flexibility
Network Effect	Minimal	Critical
Pricing	Cost-based	Value-based
Product Innovation	The big reveal	Ongoing innovation
Relationship	Ends at transaction	Forever

Table 2.1 Key Differences Between the Ownership and the Membership Economy

From Privacy to Belonging

Some people want to be anonymous, but others are willing to give up some personal information in exchange for the recognition and benefits that come from belonging. There is an ongoing and probably endless debate over the complex concept of privacy. How much private data do you want to share? And with whom? How much should you have to share in exchange for the privileges of membership? One challenge many people face is the desire to access an organization's benefits while wanting to stay independent. Some want to be protected from Big Brother, while others want to avoid superfluous social interactions. Still others are unabashed joiners and simply want to connect.

Cary Rosenzweig and I are both joiners. Maybe that's why we've both been drawn to work in the Membership Economy. Rosenzweig was the CEO for five years at IMVU, one of the first and most successful virtual worlds. According to its website, IMVU is "an online social entertainment destination where members use 3D avatars to meet new people, chat, create and play games with their friends."[1] Members can create, sell, and buy virtual goods, using virtual currency they earn through play or buy with real money.

What's fascinating about IMVU is that it's a community that encourages anonymity while still providing the benefits of membership—connection, access, and more. "One of the things that surprised me most" says Rosenzweig, "is how real the relationships and the emotions are behind the avatars."[2]

Many of the people who connected through IMVU behind the avatar facades developed genuine friendships and even met, and in at least one case married, in the real world. You see this desire to maintain privacy even while enjoying the benefits of community among younger people who use middle names as last names on social networks, or even use an alias altogether. Maybe this is for security, although most membership organizations report very few privacy violations or harassment cases. Maybe it's to hide wild behavior from schools and employers. Or maybe it's just a way to test the community before making themselves vulnerable.

A Membership Economy business model may be right for your business, even if it isn't right for you personally. You might not be a joiner—and that's okay. Nonjoiners might pay cash and forgo loyalty programs to maintain privacy about how they spend. They tend to stay away from Facebook, not just because they don't want to post, but because they find their connections' incessant sharing annoying. Membership is about connection and access over privacy and ownership—and not everyone values these the same way.

> What makes a good marketer is an interest in what motivates target buyers, how they buy, and what earns their loyalty.

Even if you are not a joiner, hundreds—if not thousands—of organizations are using the ideas, strategies, and techniques this book describes. You may not have children, but as a marketer you can sell diapers and help other people see the value of this. I have advised organizations selling high-performance bicycles, databases, and business process management software—products for which I was not the target buyer. Running a business does not mean that you become its target buyer.

What makes a good marketer is an interest in what motivates target buyers, how they buy, and what earns their loyalty. So even if membership is not for you, and you personally feel you are already too exposed, too public, and sharing too much, remember that for others membership is hugely important and worth paying a premium for.

The Membership Economy Matters to the Members

Members love membership models because they fulfill powerful human drives—like needs for affiliation and prestige.

You can certainly get all these benefits through ownership as well. Membership models, however, with their emphasis on ongoing relationships, access over owner-ship, and drip-payment plans that replace big price tags, are optimized to provide these benefits.

> *The benefits of ownership center around security, privacy, and control.*

The pendulum swings back and forth between ownership and membership. Both models can exist simultaneously, although usually one or the other is typically in a more dominant role for any given industry. The benefits of ownership center around security, privacy, and control. Right now, however, ownership is dramatically losing favor, while connection is becoming critically important. Realtors will point out that key buyer segments today are less interested in big private estates and more interested in the quality of community and shared assets like pools, clubhouses, and proximity to local attractions. Music lovers are tossing their CD collections in exchange for access to digital music subscriptions, peer-influenced discovery, and sharing communities.

Over the past 20 years, many traditional membership models have become less central to people's lives. People are more transient, both personally and in their work, which drives loneliness and vulnerability. Technology enables important connections.

The Membership Economy matters to organizations of all sizes in dozens of industries for at least three major reasons:

- *It creates recurring revenue and removes lumpiness.* Most businesses have to deal with seasonality—some more than others. Having monthly subscription revenue can smooth out the peaks and valleys in annual sales.
- *It builds a more direct relationship* that strengthens the brand, by putting customers at the organization's center. An organization that has a strong, positive relationship with its members is able to use that loyalty to grow as members recommend the enterprise to others and to resist competitive threats.
- *It generates an ongoing data stream* that can be used to improve services and identify opportunities to increase satisfaction. The more the organization understands its customers' needs, wants, behaviors, and attitudes—that is, much more than their raw demographics—the better it can serve those needs.

Virtually any organization can become part of the Membership Economy. Membership strengthens loyalty. Membership strengthens participation. Membership strengthens referrals. And organizations that think about membership tend to focus more on providing long-term value, which ultimately leads to better customer lifetime value. Any CEO who is not thinking about membership is missing a huge opportunity to point his or her organization toward long-term, sustainable profitability.

Remember

There are benefits to ownership, but today's consumers are increasingly interested in access over ownership. Access minimizes the stress of caring for and storing all our stuff, while offering us new ways to feel part of a community.

To be part of the Membership Economy, people need to face the fact that privacy of personal information may well need to be given up in exchange for the benefits of membership.

The membership model fills powerful human drives—one of the reasons it is growing in popularity among many kinds of businesses. Virtually any organization can become part of the Membership Economy.

3 The Many Faces of the Membership Economy

Membership as an organizational structure has been around for a couple thousand years. Think of the Catholic Church or the medieval guilds.

The Membership Economy, however, is a new idea enabled by the technological transformation that is sweeping the world, a result of the personal computer, the Internet, social networks, user-generated content, smartphones, cloud computing, big data, and more.

Membership is the future of all business models, with an emphasis on formal, ongoing relationships. I believe it is replacing the transactional model, and organizations that don't evolve will fail.

When you buy a product, say a pair of Nine West shoes at Nordstrom, you get a lot of help in the store, but once the transaction is completed, the relationship is over. You can choose to engage with that store again, or you can just fade away and stop coming back. There's no ongoing commitment. But with membership, you're committed until you cancel—you have to break up to end it.

> The membership model can benefit almost every organization, from the smallest mom-and-pop to the largest blue chip.

I began to notice the first stirrings of the Membership Economy 15 years ago, and I now see it everywhere. Technology was enabling new relationships between individuals, between individuals and organizations, and between organizations. As a result, certain organizations were putting customers at the center of an ongoing, formal relationship; they were able to establish what amounts to a forever transaction with their members.

A Membership Economy organization is any enterprise in which members have an ongoing and formal stake in the organization. The stake could be a subscription, as with Netflix or SurveyMonkey, or a user ID like Facebook, or a membership card like Gold's Gym. In all cases, members understand that the relationship is ongoing, not simply a transaction. Until the member cancels, the first transaction lasts forever.

In addition, in most Membership Economy organizations, the members have a responsibility to provide something—membership dues to an association or country club, content as with Pinterest or Twitter, or even just personal information as with Groupon—in exchange for access to the membership benefits. Membership Economy organizations run across a broad spectrum. The level of expression and contribution of members can grow from simply an ongoing payment model (*New York Times*) or a loyalty card (Starbucks, United Mileage Plus) to a deeply engaged group of individuals collectively molding the services the organization provides (Breast Cancer Advocacy Network's online community).

And ideally members are given the opportunity to engage not only with the organization but with one another. This means that the community as a whole benefits from the thoughts, experiences, and opinions of each member. While not all memberships include elements of community, many get big benefits from them.

Membership Economy organizations enjoy competitive advantages. Their members tend to be loyal and are likely to engage in recruiting other members. In addition, member feedback and the ongoing behavioral data members generate enable Membership Economy organizations to really understand what their members want. The closer they are to their customers, the better able they are to fend off competitive threats. If they stay locked in transactional relationships, they are vulnerable because it is more difficult to build an ongoing relationship. Members enjoy convenience, access, and flexibility.

Membership is the Holy Grail of business because recurring revenue is predictable and smooth. Smooth revenue makes it easier to manage a business, to justify additional investment, and to plan for the future. I am writing a book about the organizations that have found the Grail so others can do it too.

Membership Organizations Come in a Variety of Flavors

If Membership Economy organizations include more than nonprofits, what are some examples? Throughout this book, I focus on six types of organizations, including nonprofits. These are not the only types, and there are certainly hybrids, but if you understand the strategies and structures of these, you'll have a strong understanding of how to apply the principles anywhere. The types I spend time on are:

- *Digital subscriptions.* Online businesses in which members pay a recurring fee in exchange for access to content, features, or services. Often these are built on a "freemium" model, in which some members have a free subscription while others pay for additional benefits. Examples include Egnyte, Netflix, Pandora, and Dropbox, as well as all software-as-a-service businesses.
- *Online communities.* Group-based networks of people with shared interests or goals. Members of the same community may or may not have a social network of personal relationships as well—the primary connection is the shared interests. Many online communities leverage digital subscriptions as well. Examples include LinkedIn, Facebook, and Pinterest.

- *Loyalty programs.* Formal programs designed to track and reward loyalty and ongoing commitment, often by conferring membership status on transactional customers. Examples include Starbucks and Caesars Entertainment, as well as frequent flier programs and punch cards.
- *Traditional Membership Economy companies.* These for-profit blue chip organizations were built for membership and are frequently presented as role models for membership. Examples include American Express, T-Mobile, Curves gym, and Weight Watchers.
- *Small businesses and consultancies.* Sole proprietorships and local retailers that have incorporated Membership Economy principles into their business models. Examples include Million Dollar Consultant Alan Weiss, Kepler's Books, and the many small businesses building connections with their customers through loyalty programs, subscriptions, and online communities.
- *Nonprofits, professional societies, and trade associations.* Organizations such as professional associations, causes, religious institutions, and artistic centers that reinvest surplus revenues to achieve goals rather than distributing them as profit or dividends. Examples include the Sierra Club, AARP, and Association of Professional Photo Organizers (APPO).

The Darker Side of the Membership Economy

Some people say that the benefits of membership come at a price. Many have complained about memberships—often with good reason. Not everyone is comfortable giving up privacy. The pressure of online communities can be staggering too.

"Fear of missing out" or FOMO has made life difficult for teenagers addicted to their social networks. Others express frustration at having to pay monthly for something they only use occasionally. There have been investigations into the integrity of privacy programs among communities. And some of the most successful and beloved Membership Economy companies, like Facebook, have been accused of using member data for unapproved research.[1]

The Membership Economy doesn't cause social evils, but it brings many of them into the brave new worlds of online communities and social networks, where data can be used without permission, and an unfounded rumor can spread at lightning speed.

Remember

The Membership Economy model, enabled by technological transformation and emphasizing ongoing relationships rather than individual transactions, can benefit almost every organization. Membership makes recurring revenue predictable and smooth.

Membership Economy organizations can be structured as digital subscriptions, online communities, loyalty programs, traditional Membership Economy companies, small business and consultancies, or nonprofits/trade associations.

The Membership Economy is not without its troubling aspects, such as relinquishing personal privacy in exchange for access, increasing the psychological burden of "fear of missing out," and the integrity of some companies. The Membership Economy does not create these social evils, but it brings them into this emerging business model.

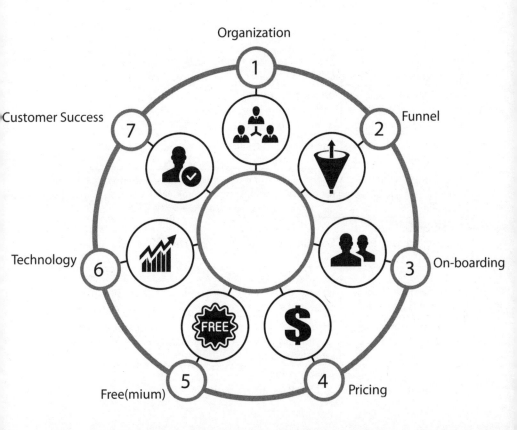

Organization

1

Customer Success

7

Funnel

2

Technology

6

On-boarding

3

Free(mium)

5

Pricing

4

Now that you've read Section I, What You Need to Know About the Membership Economy, you probably want to know how to make it work for your organization. You're ready to explore the strategies and tactics that will help you join the Membership Economy. Or, if you are already part of the Membership Economy, maybe now you're ready to up your game. If that's so, then this next section is for you, because here I teach you about the strategies that can help you.

This section is the meat and potatoes of the book. If there were a test on the Membership Economy, most of the answers would be found in this section. In this section, we look at the seven strategies outlined in Table II that form the foundation of the Membership Economy. We also look at some frontline tactics that you can apply.

As you read, keep in mind which are your favorites and which you might be able to apply right now. You might want to keep a list while you're reading. If you really understand how to apply each of these strategies, you will be well on your way to success!

Strategy	Rationale
Build the right organization	The Membership Economy requires a change in culture and attitude, not just marketing tactics.
Build an effective acquisition funnel from the bottom up	With a forever transaction, retention becomes more important than acquisition, especially since it's so much more cost effective.
Onboard members for success and superusers	The first few days for any member are critical to their long-term engagement.
Start simple with pricing, but model for flexibility	There is a fine line between options creating choice and too many options creating work. With memberships, the risk is too much complexity too early in the relationship.
Incorporate "free" as a tactic, not a strategy	"Free" can be a powerful tool in the Membership Economy, but only if it supports the overall business model.
Use the right technology and track the right data	Memberships can leave a huge trail of data—and by analyzing and acting on that information, organizations can build stronger relationships with their members.
Retain members (but know when to let them go)	Loyalty is critical in the Membership Economy, when retention drives success—but sometimes, it's better to let members go.

Table II Strategies of the Membership Economy

4

Build the Right Organization

If you want your organization to truly be part of the Membership Economy, start with the team and the culture. You need to have the right people and prioritize the right values.

Membership is at the heart of AARP. Dedicated to a mission that promises "to enhance the quality of life for all as we age, leading positive social change and delivering value to members through information, advocacy and service," the AARP truly focuses on needs of members over any other goal. In fall 2014, I met with Kevin Donnellan, AARP Executive VP and Chief of Staff and his colleague, Senior VP, Membership, Lynn Mento. They were about to launch the RealPad by AARP, a new tablet device that the AARP had developed from the ground up for "tech shy" people over 50.

I asked them how they would feel if copycat products by companies like Amazon, Samsung, and Apple were to flood the market. Their answer surprised and impressed me. "We would be thrilled," said Donnellan.[1] I was skeptical, thinking that they'd surely be frustrated about the competition. Donnellan and Mento explained that giving more choices to people 50+ was their reason for existing, and that they truly judged their organizational success by achieving that mission, rather than short-term revenue impact. This kind of mission-driven organization exemplifies the culture of the Membership Economy. When an organization wants to have a long-term relationship, they can't be blinded by short-term financial metrics.

Of course, nearly every organization admonishes employees to put the member at the center of all decisions. But there's a lot more to consider. Communication is critical; the language used in the organization when talking about members really matters. And, most importantly, marketing and innovation need to be priorities.

Promote a Culture of Marketing Innovation

Organizations dramatically underspend on marketing, research, analysis, and planning, thinking they are doing enough just because they can check the boxes around key types of campaigns and activities. (Website refresh? Check. Newsletter? Check. Loyalty program? Check.) It's not enough to do the campaigns and treat the marketing department like an outside agency. Organizations need to constantly confirm that they are reaching the right people with the right campaigns for the right offerings—and using the metrics that track long-term relationships with customers. Marketing is more than campaigns—it's about focusing on the market. This is always true, but especially in the Membership Economy, where retention matters more than acquisition.

Marketing should ensure that the offerings the organizations create meet the ongoing requirements of the target buyers and that those prospective buyers know about the benefits of the offering, sign up, and become loyal. Each of these goals has metrics, and marketing should be tracking them to be sure it is building the right kind of relationships.

Good marketing is honest. Sometimes people have the idea that good marketing is about tricking people into buying things they don't need. Not only is this approach unethical, but in the Membership Economy, with the need for ongoing relationships, it simply doesn't work.

Gainsight, a Silicon Valley technology company, provides an excellent example of the mindset needed to succeed in the Membership Economy. Gainsight has made its mission ensuring "customer success" for its subscribers. Its software helps organizations in the Membership Economy strengthen ongoing relationships with their members. CEO Nick Mehta believes that you shouldn't have a customer satisfaction department; you shouldn't have a customer support department; you should have a customer *success* department. All employees need to be empowered to make a difference, and Nick follows these guidelines in his own company, giving his team members latitude to take care of his customers.

In contrast, think about the typical customer service call: "I didn't get what I ordered," or, "It arrived broken," or, "I'm not happy with the way it works," or some variant. Organizations often train customer support people to get callers off the phone as quickly as possible. Companies sometimes measure performance by the number of calls fielded.

Customer *success*-oriented employees will be more consultative. Their task is to help callers use the product—more effectively, more efficiently—so that they will be increasingly loyal. A staff that supports customer success builds loyalty. Gainsight's mission of customer success supports the Membership Economy with its emphasis on the role of the people and the culture.

> *The entire organization needs to be aligned with the membership strategy.*

Frontline, operational employees who work for membership businesses need to understand that their unique business model depends on intimate, lasting relationships with members that often go well beyond the expectations of typical customers. This starts with employees using a personal touch with members, calling them by name, but it goes further. Customer support needs to be given more latitude and training (and probably more pay) so that the front line is fully equipped to build rapport with members and to resolve issues and concerns as they arise. Product developers and managers need to carefully consider product changes that might disrupt current member expectations. The entire organization needs to be aligned with the membership strategy.

Another role that can be useful in the Membership Economy is that of "community manager," the person who attracts, manages, and leverages the powerful community that can develop around an organization. Tim McDonald, former director of community at news community website Huffington Post and founder of My Community Manager (myCMGR.com), a community for community managers, says that the community manager needs to be both "the voice of the brand to the community and voice of the community to the brand."[2] The challenge is keeping the business's best interest in mind, while tapping into what the community says. Having a dedicated person to connect with and manage the community can pay dividends, not just in building loyalty, but also in gleaning insights about what members value in the offering.

Building a membership organization isn't just about the offering, the execution, and the product. It's also about the culture. It's about all the people you hire and how you acculturate them; what you expect from them.

To succeed in the Membership Economy, the organization must build a culture that is centered around the long-term evolution of the member relationship. The CEO and the head of marketing may know what the members need and how those needs change over time, but the head of HR must make sure that everybody believes it and lives that way. Table 4.1 shows the changing roles in the Membership Economy.

For example, in an ownership economy business, it's the salespeople who are after the big contracts. In the Membership Economy, the sales department's goal is to plant hundreds of seeds and then water them, knowing that over time, they will pay off. In an ownership economy business, the support staff's goal is to minimize customer anger. In the Membership Economy, the goal is to maximize loyalty.

	Ownership Economy	Membership Economy
CEO	Product-driven	Relationship-driven
Finance	Lumpy	Smooth
Product team	Big reveal	Tinkering
Sales	Big game hunting	Farming
Support	Minimizes anger	Maximizes loyalty
Marketing	One-way communication	Two-way (or three-way) communication
IT and operations	Build custom solution, hire lots of staff, keep it all onsite and in house	Outsource what's not core; leverage the cloud; configure, don't customize

Table 4.1 Changing Roles of the Membership Economy

Staff members at Caesars Entertainment, for example, are actually empowered to do special things for special members. They can upgrade a member, comp a drink, or make an exception to a rule, usually without manager approval.

The airlines, by contrast, generally do not have as much flexibility, although there are certainly exceptions as Virgin, Southwest, and others have put a lot into differentiating themselves over the past few years. For most airlines, there are still ample opportunities to incorporate more of a "say yes" culture to complement their loyalty programs. They call what they offer a loyalty program, but they don't have the roles and culture to support true relationships with their members.

A typical conversation can go:

Airline customer service representative: Oh, I see you have 14,513 points. You're eligible for a free first-class upgrade.
Customer: I don't want a first-class upgrade. I want my daughter on this flight with me.
Airline customer service representative: We don't do that.

Nobody is empowered to actually help a recognized member.

Not long ago I talked with a venture capitalist who invests only in subscription businesses. One of the things he said that surprised him is the very different organizational structure needed for Membership Economy enterprises. These new enterprises have a different staffing model. They have different titles. They need a different set of skills. Some people will become redundant, and some other people will need to be hired when an organization transitions to a Membership Economy model.

Membership Economy organizations need to extend the relationship with their members to partners. Relationships with developers, vendors, and suppliers in the broader community can be structured to provide further benefit for members. For example, early on, Salesforce.com invested in building a community of vendors of related products who were developing apps that extended the value of being a Salesforce.com user.

Today, Salesforce.com has a whole team of professionals who recruit, vet, and publicize these app developers in the broader Salesforce community. As a result, Salesforce users are even more entrenched in Salesforce-related products, thus increasing the value of their membership while also increasing *switching costs*. And the developers in the greater community, not the salesforce community itself, participated in the vast majority of investment in this initiative.

Commit to Continuous Innovation Supported by Marketing Insights

Innovation is motherhood and apple pie in nearly every type of organization, but for the Membership Economy, continuous innovation is especially important. The best Membership Economy organizations are constantly tinkering with their offerings. For example, American Express has offered all kinds of evolving benefits to its members over the past several years, ranging from discounts to exclusive access to special services. And Amazon continues to add features to its prime membership.

Innovation is not an event. It's a process which needs to be ingrained in an organization's culture. Innovation is described as the act of introducing new ideas, devices, or methods. In the Membership Economy, innovation is continuous. It must be, because the relationships are continuous. Most organizations think of innovations as nouns, as in, "This innovation really differentiates us from the competition." But it needs to be thought of as a verb. Organizations need to innovate constantly and always look for new and better ways to provide value.

Still, membership organizations often fail because of their lack of tinkering. Here's a complaint I've heard from leadership more than once. In this case, the executive director of a well-known nonprofit for children told me, "Members just don't behave the way they used to. They expect more from our organization. What's wrong with them, and why are they so selfish?"

For this executive director, the changing attitudes of new members were surprising and frustrating. But change is inevitable, and organizations need to assume that constant innovation is the norm. Too many organizations demonstrate an unwillingness to tinker and to be flexible. Many organizations invest heavily in a single big effort to set up a program to bring in members and then rely on it. Think of NPR with its pledge drives. It has only recently begun tinkering with 48-hour "double your pledge drives," which are short and sweet—responding to member feedback. And there are always dozens of other ways to attract and retain members.

> Members are more forgiving than customers with regard to their loyalty.

Once you bring in a new member, the member is likely to stay for a long time. And since retention is so important to revenue, it sometimes becomes the only thing organizations really focus on. So unless you are tracking new member acquisition as carefully as you track overall revenue, you might find yourself with an aging population—and no awareness or relevance to prospective members. Constant tinkering to bring in new members while retaining the ones already there can minimize this risk.

Members are more forgiving than customers with regard to their loyalty. Every time a customer transacts with an organization, customers have to make a decision to open their wallet and engage with the organization. But with membership, payments are automatic, and it's the act of unsubscription that requires an action. As a result, members stay engaged much longer than transactional customers.

Subscriptions can lull organizations into a false sense of security, convincing them that they don't need to adjust their offering or improve service because the members seem happy. However, at some point, if the discrepancy between the value the enterprise offers and the price charged becomes too great, not only does the organization lose existing members, but it also struggles to bring in new members. This kind of stumble can mean months, if not years, of poor results.

When people find out that I am an expert in subscription and membership businesses, they immediately want to tell me about the most unfair memberships they have encountered. They tell me about their frustrations as children signing up for BMG and Columbia's music clubs long ago. (Remember? Those clubs sent unrequested CDs you had to keep unless you returned them within a tight timeframe.) Or they'll complain about how the airline loyalty programs actually reduce loyalty. More recently, we've seen complaints about software companies that stopped selling packaged software the buyer can use for years in favor of monthly "subscriptions" that customers feel provide no additional value.

The fundamentals are what they always were: the customer-company relationship is based on good value in exchange for a fair price. You simply cannot run a long-term successful business if you don't seek to improve the condition of your customers and members constantly.

Your organization should have someone strategically managing your product and marketing teams who intimately understands your buyers *and* your offerings, and who can explain how and why people choose to be loyal to you, as well as how and why to find new members. If this is not who's onboard now, you may need to think about staffing changes. If you don't know, consider bringing in an outside expert to evaluate your organization. Understanding the market need and environment is the single biggest determinant of a Membership Economy organization's success.

Why Marketing Loves Membership

If you're in marketing and sales, membership makes your job easier. You have to make only a single transaction to win a customer for life. If your model incorporates community and connections, the members will build loyalty themselves. Subscription payments further fuel long-term relationships.

> Membership is not a fixture to be taken for granted.

Many membership organizations make the mistake of confusing retention dollars with new revenue. New revenue means the buyer made a decision based on today's offer. Recurring revenue is passive. A membership or subscription cancellation is a sign of active displeasure. Innovation (or lack of innovation) can be seen in these two metrics— new members and lost members.

Membership is not a fixture to be taken for granted. You can't just say, "There it is." You need to be willing to tinker. Ironically, loyalty of members can lull membership organizations into thinking that their members are happy, when actually the offering is not providing the same value it once did, and organizations haven't evolved the programming to keep up with the brand promise. One day the member "looks up," maybe because her credit card expired or because she read something in the paper, and she realizes that her subscription is worthless.

A great example is AOL.

Initially AOL, with its friendly user interface and "walled garden" model, was a safe and comfortable introduction to the Internet. Over time many other offerings began providing a much cheaper (and faster, with broadband) point of access to the Internet. The Internet itself became easier to navigate because of great new browsers.

There was a point when people in the know knew that anyone who was an AOL customer probably just didn't understand that there were much better products and deals out there. When AOL customers realized it, they felt AOL had been cheating them. AOL's brand suffered and never really recovered. This is unfortunate, since AOL was really the first major brand on the Internet. It could have become a long-term success like Google or eBay or Facebook. Instead, in 2014, it is still trying to figure out who it is—having sold off or franchised most of its technology and evolved into a brand company that owns several content properties including TechCrunch, The Huffington Post, Moviefone, and MapQuest.

There's a pull, which I have seen, between expanding a firm's offering to provide great benefit and "sticking to your knitting." eBay has tried many times to expand the utility of its huge and engaged community of merchants and traders. In 2005, eBay bought Skype for $2.6 billion, expecting that the voice-over-Internet protocol (VoIP) service would improve communications between its customers. Buyers could talk with sellers about items in which they were interested; sellers could build relationships with buyers via VoIP chats.

What eBay found, however, was that members were already comfortable using email and didn't need voice or video. And even though there was tremendous overlap in target users, it turned out that people didn't want to buy their audio/video communication service from their online marketplace. While eBay thought that there would be synergy between the two companies, the truth was that eBay members weren't interested. Four years after buying Skype, eBay sold it in 2009 for $1.9 billion. eBay has since made many acquisitions, mostly better aligned with the eBay shopping and paying experience, and these have been generally more successful.

I encourage clients to explore expansion and creative tinkering even if they still decide to stick to their knitting because I see what happens when they don't explore. If your product is really building traction—by all means, stick with it and don't dilute your focus. But when you start to see acquisition slow, or, worse, you see retention decline, you might need to consider other offers. And it's always worth exploring ways to provide increased value for loyal members.

Remember

If you want to be a true Membership Economy company for all the benefits it offers, you need to promote a culture of marketing innovation and technology. You need to use the language of membership. You need to empower your frontline staff to be able to recognize your members as individuals and take good care of them. You need to invest in your community and the people to manage the relationships and ensure their success. You need to compensate salespeople on the basis of customer lifetime value, not transactions, and you might need to rethink customer satisfaction and support.

5

Build an Effective Acquisition Funnel from the Bottom Up

Suppose I told you I didn't like McDonald's because my husband and I went there for our anniversary and were disappointed by the ambiance and lack of caviar and champagne. You might say, "Robbie, don't you know that McDonald's is not designed for wedding anniversaries? It's designed to be quick, cheap, and consistent."

McDonald's has done a great job of letting people know what its brand represents. More than that, it has done a great job of building a consistent experience. You can walk into any McDonald's in the world and know the fries will taste like McDonald's fries and the Big Mac will taste like a McDonald's Big Mac.

What's important about this clear message is that you don't have a lot of people who have experiences that were inconsistent with their expectations who then bad-mouth the product. There is some waste at the top of the McDonald's "sales funnel," in that many people who are familiar with the brand and ads would never eat there, but I think it's safe to say that few people are surprised by what they find when they walk into a McDonald's restaurant.

In this chapter, we focus on the funnel. I explain what a funnel is and how you can use a funnel or alternative structure to attract the right people, engage them, and even motivate them to strengthen the funnel by attracting and retaining others. The best Membership Economy models go beyond the transaction, tracking behaviors including sign-ups for additional services and levels of membership. The funnel can even track referrals made by existing members that lead to new members.

The Steps in a Typical Sales Acquisition Funnel

Figure 5.1 shows a typical sales acquisition funnel. Tracking the steps in your organization's funnel is important because it can provide insight into how you win (and don't win) new members.

Figure 5.1 Sales acquisition funnel.

At the top are people who are aware of the brand but haven't engaged with it yet. At the bottom are the most loyal customers. Different channels such as partnerships, ad campaigns, and events, should feed the funnel. A fraction of the people who are aware of the offering will want to learn more. Some of those people will try it. And some of the people who try it will become members. The funnel tracks individuals' progression from the moment they learn about the membership until the moment they become a member. In the middle of the funnel are prospects who have engaged with your brand but haven't become members yet. Maybe they have attended an event your organization has hosted, or they've read your newsletter. At this phase what's important is building the trust required for a formal commitment. At the bottom of the funnel are customers and their ongoing, and hopefully increasing, engagement with the organization.

Many companies are content with a wide top and a narrow bottom, the idea being that it's always good for more people to engage with you and try your product. However, funnels involve a lot of waste. Many of the people at the top who interact with your brand will never become customers and maybe *should* never become customers.

An alternative to an acquisition funnel is the chute, shown in Figure 5.2. A chute is the same width at the top and the bottom, and things move quickly from the top to the bottom of a chute. By narrowing the funnel—that is, by focusing awareness at the top and maximizing the number of prospects that stay in the funnel at each stage—an organization can have more of a chute.

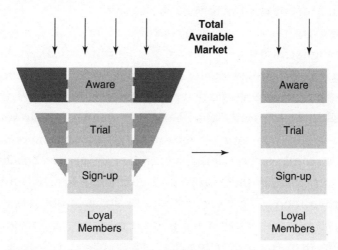

Figure 5.2 The funnel and chute.

An example of an organization that goes back and forth between funnel and chute is American Express. Initially, it started with a single card—the green one—and blanketed the marketplace with campaigns to build awareness. As the company grew more sophisticated about who actually became loyal members, it refined its awareness campaigns and also introduced new products—gold, platinum, blue, black, and most recently two new debit cards targeting people who have no existing relationship with banks, such as recent immigrants and lower income groups. As Amex introduces these new offerings and focused campaigns, they are creating multiple chutes from a single funnel.

> The important thing is to have clear definitions of each segment, and then to track the ratios.

Targeted marketing is even more important for subscription or membership businesses than for transactional organizations, because the membership organization makes a profit only if the member stays for an extended duration. So if a recurring revenue business pays for a prospect to have a free trial and the prospect is not the kind of person who would benefit from the membership, that money is wasted and the person will be disappointed with the effort.

Step 1a: Start at the Bottom of the Funnel

All efforts need to start at the bottom of the funnel, thus ensuring that there is alignment between the actual benefits provided and the target member's needs. These benefits need to align with the organization's mission, in fact, to deliver on that promise to new members. To do that, you need to know exactly who your target member is. (Do you?) You also need to be 100 percent confident that your best salesperson could convert an ideal prospect during a friendly conversation on a 45-minute plane flight. In other words, if given enough time to explain the value proposition in a customized way, the prospect would buy it.

To get value out of the funnel, first outline the steps from awareness to sign-up. In many organizations, these steps are awareness, engagement (when the prospect gives the organization permission to contact him), trial, and membership. Some funnels include postmembership sign-up events like renewal and up-selling. The important thing is to have clear definitions of each segment and then to track the ratios.

There are several ratios to track. You want to track the relationship between the number of people who are aware of your organization and the ones who engage. Then you want to track the percentage of engaged people who convert into members over a certain period of time. You probably want to track these things in a granular way—by specific campaign or channel—but as a starting point, you just want to be aware of how many people make it through each level of the funnel. If people aren't converting from one level to the next, it's like you have a hole in your funnel, and that is a waste.

Step 1b: Look Beyond the Bottom of the Funnel—Engage and Retain

Additionally, you want to be sure that members will stay once they join. This can be tricky if you are just starting out, but for established businesses, waiting to see if members stay at least for the first 30 days (long enough to establish a habit) is worthwhile. If the member/benefit alignment is strong, they will stay. You want to check because sometimes people sign up out of optimism or aspiration and then realize that they don't get any value from the membership. These people will cancel, if not now, then soon. When people cancel because they realize they aren't getting value in something they just signed up for, you can also expect that they will feel angry or betrayed. And this can convert to bad word of mouth or media publicity.

Sometimes the funnel even tracks what happens after the prospect becomes a member. By measuring how new members behave, whether they refer friends and what distinguishes the loyal ones from the ones who leave, the funnel can have greater value for membership-oriented organizations. The shape of this "funnel" resembles an *hourglass* (shown in Figure 5.3), and goes "past" the bottom of the funnel, widening to emphasize the importance of the transaction. With this funnel, you can see the impact of each individual new member in driving significant and increasing revenue after the initial transaction. If you use an hourglass funnel, you become even more aware of how important it is to retain the customers you have acquired.

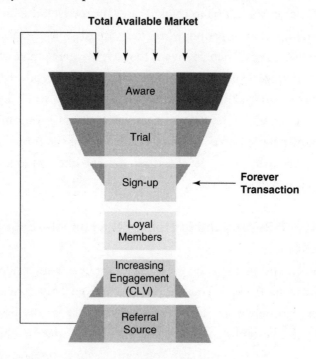

Figure 5.3 The hourglass funnel.

This is why the first step, the member/benefit alignment, is critical. If you are not certain a prospect would love the offering if he or she knew about it, there is no point in investing in anything other than fixing the offer and figuring out whom to target. Maybe you have the wrong target. Maybe the offer isn't complete.

In any case, why invest in acquiring a member who's going to leave quickly and cost you money? Membership/benefit alignment is the most important thing, but many organizations still ignore it and rush ahead to build acquisition programs.

Step 2: Refine the Message

You can't have your CEO personally deliver every pitch, so it's important to figure out how to crystallize your message so that it can be delivered without him or her. What are the key things that prospects need to know in order to engage with your organization? How can you develop the words and pictures that convey these things without an evangelist present?

You can test your message through any of your channels—on the website, through telemarketing, or in a live pitch by a telemarketer or salesperson. Testing is critical. This means trying different options in small quantities and comparing the results until you craft one that seems to work consistently.

Again, remember that you don't want to invest heavily in ads or websites or sales training for your team until you know you have the right message and offering. It is worth being patient, experimental, and flexible.

Step 3: Select Channels and Develop Programs

Now that you have a strong message, you can determine the types of campaigns to run. You want to reach prospects at a time when they're willing to buy. It doesn't matter how good your pitch is or how much I'll need a parka next winter, I'm just not going to buy one while I'm sitting on the beach in July. You need to think about the right channel and the right timing to reach your target buyers. The good thing about channels is that they are often easy to test in small iterations, so you can figure this out without big investments.

If you want to have a freemium model and rely on viral buzz, maybe you want to prioritize getting as many people as possible onto free membership to give people a chance to engage on an ongoing basis with your offerings and members. Or maybe you think you'd get better results by advertising with key words? Or through partner relationships? There are dozens of options to bring people into your funnel and nurture them until they're ready to spend money with you. What works, however, will change over time, so continue testing and measuring, even if your current approach is working.

Monitor the funnel and review the metrics at weekly team meetings to identify changes.

But remember to start at the bottom of the funnel and don't spend on acquisition until you know that prospects are likely to join, and, more importantly, to stay!

Step 4: Rinse and Repeat—Constantly

This process is not a one-time thing. It should be an ongoing activity for a membership organization because it can tell you where the challenges are. If retention is strong but acquisition is dropping, it could mean that your message is no longer compelling enough to win, even if your members demonstrate loyalty (which can be hard to distinguish from inertia). Or if you find that your retention rate is dropping, it may be there's a natural cliff where people no longer see value. Perhaps members' needs are changing.

I suggest that my clients (not just marketers, but the entire leadership team) monitor the funnel and review the metrics at weekly team meetings in order to identify changes in the ratios and also to work to improve each of these. Any time you add a new program or channel, you need to track how the metrics from that activity stack up against other programs and how you can optimize them for best results.

And remember, start at the bottom of the funnel and work your way to the top. It's a more cost-effective approach.

Continuously Improve Your Funnel—You Don't Want a Sieve

Your acquisition funnel is more than a metaphor for attracting and recruiting members. It can also tell you:

- Which channels and programs are driving awareness, acquisition, and resulting in loyal members.
- Where prospects are losing interest and disengaging from the acquisition process.
- How well your sign-up flow works.
- Where your "best" members come from.

Over time, you want to improve the conversion ratios from awareness to engagement to trial to sign-up. You can use the funnel to identify the biggest worries. For example, if you are bringing in lots of trials, but no one converts, you can focus on this step and fix it. First, develop hypotheses. Maybe people aren't fully utilizing the trial, so they don't see the benefits before the trial ends. Maybe they like the trial but find the membership terms themselves (price, duration) too high. Maybe, like one customer of mine, they didn't even realize they had signed up for the trial (evidenced by the fact that they never took advantage of the trial at all). Test these hypotheses by changing the pricing on a limited percentage of trials or by surveying the trial enrollees.

If you are investing in a significant amount of awareness activities, like email, events, tweets, and advertising, and you have a lot of people engaging with your content and members, but no one signs up for a trial, maybe they don't need your offering, but like your emails, free events, and website content—in other words, you are marketing to the wrong people.

Figure out where the problems are, so you can improve the funnel.

Companies that are disciplined in their approach to innovation get a much better payoff than the ones that are eager to "just try something." An example of an organization that invested in innovation before moving up the funnel is Weight Watchers Online. It focused on the bottom of the funnel, getting the experience and the benefits right before marketing to all prospects. Even though Weight Watchers had a proven and successful offline model, the whole model had to be rethought for a digital experience, and the company took its time to build a model that was quite different.

Weight Watchers Online is the exception, however. More than ever, companies are eager to start firing before they aim because they believe that they can just see what sticks. Many companies suffer from what I call the "Steve Jobs meets Field of Dreams" problem.

Jobs was famous for pointing out that sometimes his customers couldn't provide good feedback about what they wanted, because they didn't know what they wanted until they'd seen it. Ten years ago, who knew they needed an iPhone? Who knew they needed a tablet computer? The implication for many misguided entrepreneurs is that they know better than consumers what the consumers will want and "if we build it, they will come." Sadly, 99 percent of the time, this approach fails miserably. Thinking that you can be the next Steve Jobs and simply "know" what customers need is like saying you're going to drop out of college and start a company because that's what Steve Jobs did. Just because he did it doesn't mean it's going to work for everyone.

Remember

You should build an effective acquisition funnel—or chute—from the bottom up, constantly refine the message, select the marketing channels to reach the most likely prospects at the time they are most likely to be interested in what you have to offer, and reiterate with discipline. Once you have an efficient funnel, you want to bring members on board by removing friction and delivering immediate value as well as rewarding desired behaviors that drive member success—the subject of the next chapter.

6

Onboard Members for Success and Superusers

A membership organization wants—needs—its members to make a habit of stopping by, of participating. The organization needs a strategy and tactics to encourage members to make the visit a regular habit. This starts by bringing new members on board effectively.

I encourage my clients to optimize the onboarding process even before we start to think about the acquisition funnel. Member onboarding is a lot like employee onboarding, the process of bringing people into the organization. It includes providing a road map of what to expect and helping them be successful in getting up to speed. Just as with employee onboarding, membership onboarding ensures that the member has the knowledge, habits, and cultural mindset to be successful in this new community. Onboarding begins right after someone signs up.

A successful onboarding process (shown in Table 6.1 and Figure 6.1) has three key steps:

- Removing friction
- Delivering immediate value
- Rewarding desired behaviors that will drive member success

"Rinse and repeat" these steps to convert new members into renewing members and, over time, increase their loyalty and activity in the community.

Remove Friction	
Sign-up (free trial or regular)	Make the process as frictionless as possible.
Welcome	Make sure customers know what they signed up for. Thank them for joining.
Deliver Immediate Value	
Engage immediately	Provide initial value (a song, a gift, a fact). Start a "game" (gamification) to encourage ideal behaviors. Connect with others in the community.
Ask for feedback	Call, email, or intercept within first week. Be ready to listen.
Provide feedback	Let them know how they stack up relative to other members—time, engagement, demographics. If possible, point out the unique strengths of each member.
Reward Desired Behaviors	
Ask for referrals	Encourage members to invite other friends in the first 30 days.
Begin customizing the experience using data analytics	Offer unique elements to the experience to demonstrate recognition. Focus on continuous tinkering and not the big reveal.
Transition to a nurturing program	Continue to provide information to help them optimize their experience and connect. Communicate in a consistent, ongoing way.

Table 6.1 The Onboarding Process

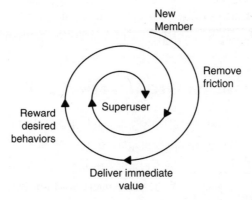

Figure 6.1 Onboarding for superusers: a virtuous cycle of three repeating steps—remove friction, deliver immediate value, and reward desired behaviors.

In the Membership Economy, the first task of onboarding is removing friction—anything that slows down a user's ability to engage with the services offered, especially during the sign-up process. The rationale for investing in removing friction is simple: You don't want to lose a potential member because any one step on the path to signing up and getting value was too hard or time-consuming.

The second step is delivering immediate value. Camille Watson, director of marketing in Netflix's early days, says it was critical that new members got a great experience right away. She remembers, "We knew members couldn't experience the full power of Netflix until they returned the first three movies and could experience the rapid turnaround in getting the next movie. So we made sure that they picked five movies up front." [1]

Pandora does this in a different way. By choosing just one single song or artist, the user gets to start listening for free to a "station" optimized around that song. Over time, you can add other songs and artists, or simply react to the songs Pandora picks with a thumbs up or down.

The third step, rewarding desired behaviors, is about building the habits of successful users of your company's value. There are significant data supporting the idea that getting someone to behave in a certain way for a certain period of time (such as 30 days) dramatically increases the likelihood that this behavior will become part of the person's regular life.

If you want trial users to become active, loyal members (and maybe eventually to become superusers), you want to acculturate them to these habits.

What Defines an Organization's Superusers

The Membership Economy values special kinds of users, superusers. They are those especially loyal and engaged members who leverage the power of the community through their participation. Superusers are members who spend significant time participating in the community. Someone becomes a superuser by building the habit of consistent group participation. It's not about single instances of heavy usage, but ongoing regular usage.

> Superusers are members who spend significant time participating in the community.

If membership is about forming habits, what kinds of habits define superusers? Here's a list of the seven habits of superusers. These are the kinds of behaviors nearly every organization wants to encourage and the fuel that will blast them forward in the Membership Economy.

Superusers . . .

1. Check in frequently and consistently—not just once a year for an intense engagement.
2. Create content that others can access.
3. "Police" the community and ensure that cultural norms that strengthen the group are enforced.
4. Have a two-way relationship with the organization itself—providing feedback and suggestions.
5. Demonstrate genuine desire to help other members.
6. Attract new members.
7. Aid in the onboarding of new members.

It is virtually impossible for a superuser to achieve this status in multiple networks and communities. There just isn't enough time for extreme engagement (which can be 20, 30, or even 40 hours per week).

So how do you increase the likelihood that your members become superusers of your organization?

Increasing the Number of Your Organization's Superusers

In studying superusers, I was lucky enough to connect with Dr. Michael Wu, the chief scientist at Lithium, a firm that "helps companies respond on social networks and build trusted content on a community they own."[2] Wu is an expert on community and memberships, but he also creates and activates social networks and communities of his own.

Wu's job is to develop theories about social networks and communities, prove these theories with data, and eventually build the product that leverages those theories for his company. His research informs and is inspired by the way Lithium's customers, some of the largest brands in the world, are building communities.

One of the most interesting things Wu brought up was an organization's ability to create loyalty through the utilization of behavioral economics. In general, Wu is more interested in timeless aspects of human behavior than he is in technology. He thinks that the role of technology is to leverage these predictable behaviors. For example, Wu said that someone becomes a superuser by having the habit of consistent group participation. It's not about heavy usage one time, but ongoing regular usage.[3] A superuser is key to the success of both social networks and communities. Wu shared his insight that organizations can design the onboarding experience to encourage superuser behavior, through gamification as well as through other strategies.

Gamification is the idea of applying game thinking and mechanics to nongame settings, usually as a motivator. Common examples include tracking points, offering status levels, and providing prizes for achieving certain levels of participation. Gamification can provide an extrinsic motivation for customers to participate until intrinsic motivation kicks in.

Gamification is a means of artificially providing value to the members before they begin to experience the authentic value of the membership. Badgeville (Badgeville.com) is an example of a company designed to help Membership Economy businesses leverage the value of membership through gamification.

Organizations reward members in different ways. Sometimes members are rewarded for helping others, as is the case with Quora, the question-and-answer website in which its community of users create, answer, edit, and organize questions, and earn points through participation. Other times, members are rewarded for achieving early milestones on their way to their goal. For example, Weight Watchers Online allocates members a certain number of points to spend on food each day, with the opportunity to earn additional points through activities. Success in weight loss in turn generates increased loyalty and word-of-mouth. Quora and Weight Watchers both use technology to leverage predictable behavior, which drives the success of their members, ultimately increasing the number of superusers among their members. While someone may initially be motivated by the person's individual goals, for example, losing weight, over time that personal motivation may evolve to be somewhat altruistic as they increasingly help others to do the same. Building in elements to encourage desired behaviors early on is critical.

Why Superusers Are Important to the Organization

A superuser is not necessarily the most profitable customer—some customers spend a lot of money without ever engaging emotionally with the company, product, or other members. However, superusers are responsible for driving a lot of value. For example, many of the most active members of LinkedIn don't pay to subscribe. And the ones who do subscribe, such as recruiters and salespeople, may not create content or invite new members to join the community.

Most organizations have a small percentage of superusers. There is a general rule among Internet communities that 90 percent of members of a community are lurkers, 9 percent contribute occasionally, and 1 percent contribute frequently. Wu's research into 143 online communities found that while his numbers varied somewhat, these ratios generally hold.[4]

> *Superusers are the key to the long-term success of any membership community.*

So why do superusers matter so much? Superusers engage, attract, and actively recruit new members. While some scientists have tried to develop methods to predict who will be a superuser, Wu hasn't been able to find any reliable data that provide a way to do so. What is possible, though, is to identify potential superusers by their similarities to other superusers and then to encourage certain behaviors.

One technique is to track the activity of all members and then look for cases in which users are checking in, reading, creating, or inviting on a more regular and frequent basis than the norm. Those people are likely to be superusers.

An organization achieves cultlike status when there is a small group of very devoted supporters who care about the organization very much—some might say too much. I think of a cult as an organization that has more than its fair share of superusers. Ultimately, this is what most organizations want to achieve. CrossFit seems to have done so.

While many exercise organizations leverage membership economy principles—that's why they're called health "clubs"—the CrossFit community has more deeply embraced the Membership Economy than nearly any other exercise organization. As a result, CrossFit has developed an intensely loyal following.

Every Tuesday and Thursday at noon, my sister and brother-in-law attend an intensive workout in an old warehouse 20 minutes from their workplaces where they grunt and sweat with 12 other members of CrossFit Palo Alto (CFPA). Together, they complete the workout of the day (WOD), which is the same WOD being completed at every CrossFit "box," what members call the rough, unfinished workout facilities. CrossFit gives scores for each activity and notes personal bests and best performers across each box. The workout is challenging, but the timing is easy—it's short and sweet—less than an hour just twice a week, and, if necessary, it can be done at home.

It's easy to get involved because once you join, there is only one program. Experienced members will welcome and indoctrinate you. Members are committed to specific workout days, teams, and times, so they get to know each other well. And, perhaps most importantly, everyone must stay and support members until all members have completed the WOD, encouraging deep, authentic connections and also motivating every athlete to work out hard and come back again to progress.

There are regular events throughout the year in which the community comes together—a holiday party, an all women's event, training seminars, a charity fund-raiser (involving climbing to the top of the Bank of America building in San Francisco), and the annual "CrossFit Open" in which CrossFitters all over the world do the same five workouts and see how they stack up against the world. There's a personal record board where everyone writes down personal successes. One of the benefits of people knowing each other is that they know to reach out and harass each other when someone doesn't show up, which is both good from a business standpoint and from a fitness effectiveness one. Members often partner up, sharing a bar for lifts, so they can encourage and teach each other. Jimi Letchford, the brand manager at CrossFit, told me, "We look at value different than other gyms. We're not about $19.99 for gym and pool access. For us it's about the coaching and community, the ability to reach a coach 24/7. People who go recognize the value of what they're getting, and that's why they are so loyal."[5]

If people are referring to your nonreligious organization as a cult, chances are you are building tremendous engagement and loyalty. I find it interesting that people use the language of religious extremists in describing organizations that have strong followings of superusers. For example, many refer to the CrossFit gym as the "Church of the Holy CrossFit" or refer to "technology evangelists" who resemble missionaries in their efforts to convert new members.

Companies like CrossFit follow three rules to drive loyalty:

- Make it easy.
- Make it personal.
- Get members involved.

These three rules are discussed in more detail in Chapter 10, How to Retain Members (and When to Let Them Go).

To create superusers, make achievement of goals part of onboarding and of the ongoing member experience.

Techniques for Onboarding That Create Superusers

Gamification exemplifies the three rules of driving loyalty. An example of this is built into Kurbo's pediatric weight loss program. Kurbo is the first comprehensive adolescent weight loss program to combine the flexibility of mobile technology with the customization of personal coaches. As new members play games to learn which foods to eat, they gain points and status. These activities are especially heavy in the first few weeks of membership—both to build habits and to motivate the children until the weight loss itself kicks in, providing more organic incentives.[6] Kurbo's approach is easy, personal, and involving.

A robust loyalty program can be another way to leverage the three rules of driving loyalty. Caesars Entertainment Corporation (known as Harrah's Entertainment from 1995 to 2010) invests heavily in onboarding new members of its TotalRewards program, which is profiled in Chapter 13, What You Can Learn from Loyalty Programs. Caesars provides members a differentiated experience with meaningful benefits from the moment they sign up. (An example of making it easy.) Caesars empowers its frontline employees to use member data to "make it personal" for each guest enrolled in the TotalRewards program. Caesars has worked hard to create customized relationships with members, an example of getting members involved.

Risks Come with Superusers

As with nearly any good thing, superusers also have downsides. Most of the time, your heaviest users want to strengthen the community. Sometimes though, there are super(evil)users. These people participate heavily in the community, but in a way that poisons members. In gamer-based membership organizations, there are people known as griefers who take pleasure in wrecking game dynamics.

Sometimes even well-meaning superusers can distract the team with their demands. Dawn Sweeney, CEO of the National Restaurant Association, one of the largest and most influential business trade associations, pointed out to me that many professional associations end up with lopsided organizations that represent only a fraction of their mandated mission because a few overzealous superusers push for benefits that appeal to the minority. These members may think they're voicing the wishes of the masses and not realize their own biases.[7]

Subscription-driven content models like Gamefly and Netflix need to be mindful of active users who regularly write negative reviews. They can do this by setting guidelines and expectations up front, and by quickly taking action against participants who do not have the organization's best interests at heart. Critical content can anger the publishers and producers, who are important partners. In addition, negative comments can change consumer behavior, resulting in peaks and valleys in content use. Many organizations have avoided reviews and community engagement entirely out of fear of biasing consumers.

> *Ultimately Mixx failed because it wasn't able to adjust quickly enough to the competing needs and demands of its users.*

Mixx, a digital news community that is one of the more interesting experiments of the Membership Economy, is a noble failure. It's an example of what can go wrong when a small group of superusers becomes too powerful. Ultimately it failed because it wasn't able to adjust quickly enough to the growth and to the competing needs and demands of its users.

The idea of Mixx was that all members had a home page to post their own high-interest news. So a single page might be a mix of Red Sox coverage, D.C./politics, and Alzheimer's research. Members could discover, share, and comment on posted news.

At Mixx, the product team struggled with aggressive demands for new features made by superusers, but these sophisticated new features were not relevant to most members and actually resulted in lost members.

Founder Chris McGill says he created a framework and infrastructure and let the members fill it in. Mixx embraced a radical idea of membership—the idea that all the value and content in the membership would come from the members themselves, through the content they created.[8]

In hindsight, McGill says he wishes that he had done a few things differently. Early members begged for a Mixx home page that had highest trending news. Ultimately, this page became a target for spammers and political wackos, rendering it useless (and dangerous). Mixx should not have responded so often to the superuser feature requests. Mixx created turbo tools that were great for experienced, committed members, but too complicated for new folks.

For the first million users, Mixx functioned beautifully. But at critical mass, the whole site changed. People who wanted to take advantage of the site's popularity moved in. Spammers would mask messages and submit spam to sites (think online workers in India submitting spam for $2/day). Nutcases with political agendas moved in, and both the spammers and the extremists hurt the product.

In his prior role as vice president of strategy at *USA TODAY*, all McGill wanted to do was to give consumers a voice in what was said without running over the journalists. He sees it as a noble mission not just for the business, but for the United States as a whole. McGill learned firsthand, however, how hard it is to manage a true democracy. "It doesn't take a lot of rotten apples to spoil the batch."

One of the problems with social media is that things have to trend before they rise to the top—that's the problem with breaking news on a social news site. Using Digg, it would be a while before breaking news surfaced. Mixx solved this problem by giving its superusers, known as SuperMixxers, extra power. If two SuperMixxers marked something as "breaking," it would rise immediately.

Eventually, the SuperMixxers grew too powerful. The site suffered from feature creep and became too complicated. McGill looks back on his time with Mixx very fondly—justifiably proud of his radical experiment in membership "To this day, I love those guys," he says. "What we built was fabulous for the SuperMixxers, even though it was confusing for others."

McGill was a true pioneer. He believes that Mixx was more than just a "better business model. It was important for the country. We didn't have a voice, we were being run over by money and politics . . . we needed a forum in which it wasn't radical chaos."

Focusing on building superusers can result in a much stronger organization. Superusers are the flywheel for many Membership Economy companies. They are responsible for causing a viral *network effect*, content creation, and peer support and sharing. Also, by carefully cultivating superusers, an enterprise can make itself more valuable to all users. However, it can be challenging to manage superusers, which can create tremendous risk.

Remember

The onboarding process is crucial for a Membership Economy organization's success. The task has to be as friction-free as possible and immediately engaging. The organization should ask for and offer feedback, ask for referrals, and begin customizing members' experience using data analytics. The goal, after all, is to create a band of superusers who have almost a cultlike attachment to the enterprise. And of course, you want to charge enough to make the whole effort profitable while not charging so much that you discourage membership.

7

Start Simple with Pricing, but Leave Room for Flexibility

Pricing is hard to get right, but it's critical to the success and longevity of virtually every organization. Pricing is especially tricky in the Membership Economy because instead of pricing widgets, organizations need to price ongoing experiences and perceived value.

Pricing is critical because money drives the economy. Even nonprofits need to manage this scarce and limited resource. Throughout time, vendors have determined the price of a product or service in two primary ways:

- The cost of making the product or supplying the service
- The perceived value of the product or service

If I sell you a chicken, I could set the price based on what it cost me to raise the chicken, kill the chicken, and deliver it to your house. Or I could set the price based on what I think you might pay for it.

And if you have a real hankering for chicken and I have the only one in town, you might pay considerably more than what it cost me to raise and prepare it.

Why Pricing Is Important to the Membership Economy

Pricing is important to the Membership Economy because making revenue less lumpy and more predictable is a key benefit of ongoing relationships. Pricing for membership is not as easy as charging $10 for a product that cost $5 to manufacture. Indeed, enterprises in the Membership Economy employ a number of pricing concepts:

- The value needs to be clear and differentiated.
- The organization needs to change the product and service offerings to stay current with the times.
- The pricing needs to be transparent.

Membership models are very attractive to organizations, and recurring revenue models can be enticing. If you are not providing ongoing benefits to justify the ongoing payments, however, your business model is likely to fail.

Seven Potential Revenue Streams

Most membership businesses start and end their exploration of revenue stream creation with their subscription models. And to be fair, building a solid subscription model with multiple *pricing tiers* requires creativity, discipline, and rigorous analysis. However, selling subscriptions is just one way to charge members for value created. I have identified six tactics in addition to—or that can supplement—subscription models. But let's start with subscriptions.

1. Subscriptions

Because a membership almost by definition provides ongoing value for members for the duration of the membership, the vast majority of membership organizations offer a subscription payment model.

While some organizations have only a single subscription price and offering, tiered pricing offers greater flexibility and options. Most organizations aim to have three options, taking advantage of pricing research that indicates that most people prefer to have multiple options, that three is the right number of choices, and that the majority prefers the middle option.

> *Market the benefits of upgrading to people at the lower levels.*

In cases where the tiers are based on target buyer demographics (for example, students, individuals, corporations), it is unlikely that upgrades will be frequent, but in other cases, where the tiers are based on usage patterns and preferences, it is critical to think through what drives conversion behavior. It's important to market the benefits of upgrading to people at the lower levels so that they have good reason to convert.

Often subscriptions have low variable costs because they provide members access to shared resources such as content, events, or durable goods. In these cases, pricing is based on the value provided to customers, as well as the cost of alternatives.

With some subscriptions, however, it can be hard to predict the cost of delivery. You don't know how much people will actually use the service, and usage changes over time. Data have enabled companies to get much closer to understanding the actual costs, though. Subscription-based businesses build complex algorithms to determine the average cost of serving their members, which can inform pricing.

With subscriptions, it's always better to price based on the value the organization provides to the member. When you price for value, you focus on what the member wants, which is best for everyone. The challenge comes when the perceived and actual needs of the member change over time—which they always do. Pricing consistently and fairly over time needs to be a core expertise of any membership organization. Tinkering is important, and connecting to the market is critical. As a result, pricing quickly gets complicated.

Most subscription-based businesses grapple with the question of payment frequency. Should it be weekly? Monthly? Annually? The only way to know is to test; you cannot pick the most effective frequency out of the ozone. For many businesses, an annual payment is best because it locks in longer terms, but these lump-sum payments often alter the decision from one of impulse and low consideration to a thoughtful, considered purchase. And once members start rethinking the purchase, they may also rethink the value, and the likelihood of cancellation rises.

Because many individuals do not analyze their subscriptions once they make the initial purchase decision—because the monthly cost does not seem worth serious consideration—organizations run the risk of assuming that members will continue to recognize the value for their investment. In fact, they are mostly oblivious.

Often, however, customers react slowly to changes in value, such as when competitors enter the market offering alternatives at a much lower price. Part of the tacit agreement between the organization and the member is that the organization will continue to modify the membership's features to stay current and to maintain the value. Otherwise, when an external event occurs that requires action by the member (such as an expired credit card, news of alternative products, or a change in policy), the members may abruptly recognize the gap between price and value, feel cheated, cancel the subscription, and, sometimes, complain publicly about the organization. While subscribers tend to be very loyal for the duration of their membership, often they are the angriest ex-customers.

2. À La Carte Services

À la carte services are out-of-the-ordinary services members do not require on an ongoing basis—for example, a one-time indexing of your content, or an on boarding fee, or a health audit at the gym.

A mistake many organizations make is to put this type of one-time service into a higher-level, ongoing pricing tier. The problem is that either the consumer feels gypped, being forced to pay for a whole year for a one-time need, or "games" the system, upgrading for a month to satisfy the one-time need, then dropping back to the basic membership.

Gaming the system may seem harmless, but it masks true consumer behavior, making it hard to understand the true needs of key market segments, while training consumers to look for loopholes rather than trusting the pricing to be fair.

3. Ancillary Products

Not all members need the ancillary products, but people using the subscription often buy them to enhance the ongoing service. For example, Skype sells headsets, Apple sells iPhotobooks, gyms sell shorts, and museum stores sell mementos and reference tools to enhance the museum experience.

4. Partnership Streams

If your members need or are likely to want services or products that fall outside of your mission but can be served by another organization, partnerships might be a good option. Partnership streams are shared revenues or commissions provided in exchange for referrals or cross-marketing.

With ancillary products and à la carte services, the membership organization develops and sells directly to members. Partnership streams are less risky because they don't require the organization to develop products or in-house capabilities even though these can drive significant revenue. For example, many hotels feature rental car desks inside their hotels, and country clubs may offer dry-cleaning drop off and pick up while members use the facilities.

5. Aggregated Analytics

Companies often overlook aggregated analytics. Big data are the result of network effects and ongoing relationships. These data can take the form of survey results, salary data, demographic information, or behavioral data. While all organizations are able to take advantage of the incredible rise in data tracking, a membership organization has the added benefit of watching people's behavior over time.

Longitudinal data have all kinds of value—not just for the company but for individual members or for other types of organizations. For example, LinkedIn has been able to aggregate data about employees at specific companies and then provide highly useful "company profiles" that share popular titles of new hires. This can be invaluable for competitive intelligence. Or subscription billing vendors can develop best practice recommendations by comparing member onboarding, pricing, or conversion tactics across key segments like music, retail, or software.

These aggregated data are certainly valuable internally, but they often can provide additional value to existing customers, or even be a source of revenue from a totally new buying segment.

6. Advertising

There is still opportunity to generate revenue by providing access to your audiences, but it needs to fit with your business and should provide value to your audience as well. Some organizations shy away from this and tout the fact that, "We'll never sell your name or show you ads." But there is a place for advertising, especially when the audiences are extremely targeted—and this is key.

Picture yourself facing the Pacific Ocean at a "club" resort in Mexico. In the lobby are advertisements for zip lining, horseback riding, and other forms of off-property entertainment. The resort manager would say that members want these ads and flyers so that they can access good services while visiting this remote location. Customers rely on the club to limit advertisers to quality vendors, but also I assume that members understand that these vendors pay advertising fees to the club.

> Advertising as a business model is out of favor in general.

If you walk into a venture capitalist's office with an idea for a new membership organization built on an advertising model, you are unlikely to be successful. Advertising as a business model is out of favor in general. However, this is more the effect of technology's rapid change than because advertising doesn't work. After all, advertising is paid content designed to drive awareness, consideration, trial, or all three. However, there are new ways to build awareness that work much better than advertising these days. Content marketing and syndication are, on some level, forms of advertising, as are certain types of sponsorships.

7. Free

While "free" is not itself a revenue stream (in fact, it's the opposite of a revenue stream!), having free product and service offerings can drive revenue in predictable ways as we'll see in the next chapter.

When and How to Raise (or Lower) Prices

Changing pricing can be hard. I start by talking about raising prices, because that's usually the goal. Maybe you want to raise prices because your competitors charge more, and you think you should too—that's the easiest time to raise prices. Maybe because the cost of delivering the value is rising—as was the case with Netflix when it changed its pricing in 2011 in response to the movie studios' increased pricing.

With membership, there is often an implicit assumption that the dues or subscription will remain constant forever. You run the risk of spiking churn when you change prices because members may reconsider membership when prices change. To avoid the painful market backlash around raising prices, you can do a few things:

- *You can "grandfather" existing members at the old prices* and raise prices for new members only—this avoids backlash while also building *stickiness.* If people cancel and then rejoin, they lose the benefit of their lower price.
- *You can add tiers above the current level* with more benefits, and you can charge more. Then members pay the higher cost only if they want the higher level of benefit.

If you must raise prices for existing members, brace yourself. You are likely to experience a spike in churn and maybe in negative feedback. One way to minimize the impact is to be transparent about the price increase. You can also add and remove à la carte services, as people tend to be less sensitive about pricing changes in transactional, one-time expenses.

Lowering prices would seem to be easier, as people love discounts, but there are a few challenges to keep in mind. First, once you drop prices, it's very hard to raise them again, so be sure it's the right decision. Second, dropping prices can signal a drop in value or prestige to the membership. Third, it is difficult and unethical to drop prices for new members while keeping them high for the long-time, loyal members.

If your costs drop dramatically, however, or if you are facing competitive pressures, you may need to drop prices. Make sure that you position the pricing change in a positive way. Even if you have millions of members, remember that they have an ongoing relationship with you and expect (and deserve) a personal and clear explanation for the change.

The Difference Between Freemium and Giving Away the Milk

Even Membership Economy companies that use "free" to power their revenue engine must generate revenue. This is true even when the free offering is wildly successful. You just can't make it up on volume when your profit-per-unit is zero.

Nearly every company I've worked with has benefited from offering options to customers and providing different levels of membership for different segments of members. Many companies make the mistake of structuring the options before considering their objectives. Before defining the options, it's important to think about the key segments of your business, and what their needs are.

The vast majority of customers of online-survey pioneer SurveyMonkey opt for the free offering. However, SurveyMonkey offers three other options—select, gold, and platinum—each of which is designed to meet the needs of a key customer group for whom the potential value of SurveyMonkey's service is much higher. These key groups include heavy survey users, sophisticated researchers who need to export their data into analytics tools, and corporate clients who want to brand their surveys and who don't want their respondents to know that SurveyMonkey is being used. These groups are willing to pay a premium for certain features and benefits.

Generally speaking, some of the benefits offered in the more expensive tiers have direct costs associated with them, like customer support. Others have no variable costs, but because of the perceived value can command a premium. In structuring tiers for your subscription, you should consider several different levers, as summarized in Table 7.1.

Levers	Tactics
Volume	More users More storage More time More interactions
Duration	Longer access
Features	Additional products Additional tools
Service	Support Customization Implementation

Table 7.1 Levers for Developing Tiered Pricing

Volume. Many customers will pay more for access to more. They want volume. This kind of distinction is easy and obvious to deliver and is a great way to up-sell a customer from free to paid, with free serving as a trial for potential heavy users. There are a few different kinds of volume:

- *Volume of content.* For example, newspapers that offer some content for free and other higher-value content for a price.
- *Volume of users or accounts.* Many of the Twitter management services, for example, allow free management for the first few feeds and charge for more complex usage.

Duration.   Pandora limits free subscribers to a certain number of hours per month, but customers willing to pay more (or listen to ads) can get longer access.

Features.   With companies like SurveyMonkey, Zynga, and LinkedIn, users enjoy additional features when they upgrade. For example, more sophisticated analytic tools are available to SurveyMonkey pro customers. LinkedIn has been particularly aggressive about encouraging freemium subscribers to upgrade by highlighting desirable features, such as knowing who is looking at their profile, being able to search on more variables, or being able to connect with people who are outside their network. When members try to access these features by clicking on the links, LinkedIn presents a *paywall* with an opportunity to upgrade for access via an "upgrade now" link.

Service.   Organizations can offer supporting services, like help-desk and setup resources. They can also remove annoyances, such as ads. These moves make the overall experience smoother and more pleasant. One of the challenges many Membership Economy organizations encounter offering a freemium option is determining how to afford to support the offering. By charging for service usage, organizations can let their members choose whether they want to access this cost center. Support has direct variable costs, and companies need to decide if they want to pass through those costs or risk a poor user experience.

Common Pricing Mistakes

In my career I've seen companies make a number of mistakes in their pricing. Here are some of the most common:

- *Offering a discount.* The key issue in pricing is to figure out what people are willing to pay for initially, as well as what they are willing to keep paying for. Discounts on pricing need to be crafted to impact longer-term value—that is, getting people to try the product long enough and under the right circumstances so that they understand the value and commit to the full price. Discounts over time are useful if the alternative is losing the customer. For example, with weight loss, customers might be willing to pay a huge premium to lose the weight, but once the weight is gone, they may need a significant discount to participate in an ongoing, indefinite maintenance program.

> *Pricing against someone who uses a loss leader can especially hurt organizations that are perceived to be forcing customers to subscribe for more than they need.*

- *Pricing against someone who uses a loss leader.* Harvard Business School professor Clayton Christensen warns of the risk of innovation from below. Someone can come along who will provide 10 percent of the benefits at 3 percent of the price. This is a case of good enough at a great price. For example, the Skype model was originally unique—no one else was offering online video chat. But over time, Google, Apple, and others began to offer online chat for free. Skype still had some features that were better than these new entrants, but it lost a lot of customers to the free option. The same thing is happening with digital storage, with Apple, Microsoft, eBay, and Google giving away storage and sharing as a loss leader and putting pressure on organizations like Dropbox and Box. This kind of disruption can especially hurt organizations that are perceived to be forcing customers to subscribe for more than they need.

- *Pricing against someone who makes "an enthusiastic mistake."* Napster provided a platform for people to "share" their music libraries online for free. The only problem was that it was illegal. Eventually Napster was forced to stop enabling this type of sharing. However, by that time, Napster had conflated downloading digital music with "free" in the eyes of music lovers. As a result, it took years for the music industry to recover (in fact, it is still recovering) and for other companies—such as Apple and Spotify—to build traction with a business model for digital music.

■ *Pricing too low or giving it away at the outset.* If you price too low at the outset, it's hard to recover without either grandfathering in all the people who have the "good deal" or offering significant perceived value to justify the cost increase. Once you've taught customers that they should get a good price, it's hard to unteach them. Especially with membership models.

■ *Pricing too high at the outset.* While it's easier to lower prices than to raise them, if you launch with prices perceived as too high, it's hard to change people's brand perception and win people back. For example, concierge medicine was a great idea, but it was initially priced out of the reach of most consumers—now there's a company called HealthTap. For $99 a year you can get your questions answered by a doctor 24/7. You don't get the actual care and treatment of a concierge doctor, but many people are willing to pay the subscription fee and keep their traditional coverage instead of paying exorbitant costs for "private doctors."

■ *Offering too many flavors and discounts.* There is ample evidence that providing three options is optimal. If you have too many options, people are overwhelmed. Too few, and there's a risk prospects won't find one that seems to fit. But sometimes once you start segmenting, you come up with too many use cases. The three drivers of options—volume, service, and features—have limitless permutations, and it is tempting to offer hundreds of options. Look at the mobile service industry to get a sense of what can happen. T-Mobile gained market share and credibility by simplifying the plans. Keep it simple.

Remember

While pricing can be tricky in the Membership Economy, the membership model offers a number of revenue streams: subscriptions, à la carte services, ancillary products, partnership possibilities, analytics based on the data collected automatically, and advertising. Also, although raising a price is often traumatic for an enterprise, we've seen that it's possible to mitigate the negative effects. At the same time, there are a number of common pricing mistakes to avoid: pricing too high or too low, offering an inopportune discount, and more. The other challenge, of course, is knowing what to offer for free, when, and for how long.

8 | Incorporate "Free" as a Tactic, Not a Strategy

Not long ago, a friend gave me a very expensive, made-to-order olive-and-purple coat that didn't fit her correctly once it was made. Olive and purple makes my skin look gray, and the loose style makes me look like a box. But did I mention it was free? Despite the fact that I knew from the second I saw it that I would never wear it, I could not reject it. That is the power of free.

Businesses know the power of free: free razors to sell razor blades, free software trials, and free tchotchkes to lure you into booths at conventions and county fairs. Membership businesses are particularly sophisticated about free stuff. Many of the best membership businesses have a free offering that drives awareness and trial while simultaneously creating a community. Free membership creates stronger networks, which in turn attracts additional users, launching a virtuous cycle.

In many Membership Economy companies, the fixed costs are high, but the variable costs are very low—often virtually zero. This opens up all kinds of possibilities for free. Free trial is an old idea, but is attractive in the Membership Economy because of the ability to provide a taste for a limited period of time as well as to offer freemium—the subscription business model in which a free option provides ongoing value essentially forever.

Free content, or "content marketing," is the practice of providing some free information as a means of building awareness and credibility with prospective members. It's like advertising, except that the enterprise actually provides valuable content—research, news, ideas—instead of buying advertising and promotion. Other kinds of free include a free gift with purchase, a free lunch for hearing a pitch, a gift for visiting a store, a free latte for reaching a loyalty level, and more.

"Free" is not a business model; it's merely a marketing tactic that helps generate revenue and deliver profits. Many companies, especially digital businesses, launch their businesses with free or deeply discounted offerings as a means of building interest and critical mass in their enterprise. Unfortunately, only some are able to sufficiently leverage free tactics, such as free samples, freemium models, or free content, to drive revenue. We talked about free in Chapter 7, but we didn't get into specifics. Here's how the successful companies make it work.

When to Use a Free Sample or Trial

When should you offer a free sample or trial of the organization's product or service and how much should you give away?

> There's no reason why virtually any organization cannot offer something free on a regular basis.

Samples are good when companies need to educate prospects about a product's value. Costco gives you samples so you can savor how delicious products are. Content-based subscription enterprises like Netflix and Spotify give prospects a free trial so they can see how easy the system is to use and how much great content is available.

One mistake companies make is to offer a free trial that does not provide the full experience. Sometimes they feel that they have to limit the benefits of the trial because the full experience is too expensive, but they run the risk of giving prospects the wrong idea about the experience. Prospects who experience a suboptimal trial have an inaccurate and negative impression of what they'd get if they joined.

Some companies tell me that they are reluctant to offer a free trial because they fear people could fill their need for the full benefits of membership during a finite test period. For example, if an association executive wanted to conduct one in-depth survey about members' preferences and SurveyMonkey provided free trials for its premium offerings, the executive could sign up for SurveyMonkey's premium offering, conduct the survey, and then return to the free account, without ever paying for the value. In cases such as this, however, it is likely that the prospect does not need a membership—the customer needs short-term access to your services. Create a short-term membership price instead.

When "Freemium" Makes Sense

Freemium (the word is common enough that *The New York Times* now uses it without qualification) is a level of membership that delivers ongoing value without charging a price. Technology has driven the cost of providing certain kinds of memberships almost to zero. There's no reason why virtually any organization cannot offer something free on a regular basis. Freemium offers Membership Economy organizations three key benefits:

- It can build awareness and strengthen your pipeline of paying members.
- It can build a large community of members who connect with one another and provide value and prestige to key (paying) customer segments.
- It can attract new members by encouraging extended trials.

Like virtually every other tactic, "freemium" also comes with risks:

- It can cannibalize paying members.
- It can condition people to expect a free service.
- It can provide a subpar, flimsy, ineffective solution that annoys people.

Freemium can be a great tool, but it's important to remember that freemium is a means to an end—and that end, always, is revenue. Companies without a viral or networked component to their offering can still benefit from freemium as a means of driving a trial. Companies that have happy customers who eventually upgrade to a premium (paid) solution can justify a freemium model.

Having both free and paid offerings, however, can be tricky. If you offer too much value in the free offering, members have no incentive to upgrade. If you don't offer enough value, you don't attract anyone. Worse, an unsatisfactory freemium option can anger users who feel they're being forced to upgrade to get the bare minimum value. Many companies have failed because they didn't find the right balance between free and paid offerings and value.

Remember that free is not a stand-alone strategy. A free trial and freemium are marketing tactics—ones that work only in concert with other important elements. There has to be a plan to generate revenue as a result of all the giving. Table 8.1 graphically outlines the differences between free and freemium.

	Free Trial	Freemium
Who it's for	Prospects who need to experience the product before they commit	Light users
What it is	Short-term access to the full range of benefits for free	Indefinite access to a limited range of benefits for free
When it works	When it provides a taste of the benefits; and when it shows rather than tells	When the user's participation benefits the organization and other members

Where it works	When the leap from learning to buying is big and prospects need to experience the benefits	When you're trying to create a network effect, go viral, or up-sell to a paid relationship
Why to proceed with caution	If benefits are not truly ongoing, you risk giving away all the value; also can be expensive to provide the "full experience"	Fine line between too little value to be relevant and too much value to pay for higher tiers. Sometimes has variable costs, so ROI must be there
How to decide if it's for you	Do I lose prospects at the paywall? Do they tell me the price is high and they don't fully understand how the product will work? Is the product really sticky?	Is it inexpensive (or free) to provide attractive benefits to a large group? Do I need a large audience to create value for my paying members? Do my users share the product with others?

Table 8.1 Free Trial Versus Freemium

Being able to include free offerings in your business strategy is like being a restaurant chef with a stash of wild truffles. You have a unique tool to create something really special, but you run the risk of overdoing it and ending up with an attractive yet unprofitable dish. What you really want is for free to serve as a growth engine that supports your other profitable lines of business.

When Free Did Not Make Sense

Offering a freemium option to subscribers is a tactic that can be effective with a broad range of organizations. Freemium can lead to upgrades, build awareness, and even create a network effect which adds value for each new subscriber. But sometimes freemium doesn't make sense.

I have worked with several organizations that wanted to incorporate a freemium option into their business model. Often their management teams are well-acquainted with the prevailing theories about why organizations should provide value for free in order to be competitive. In some cases, these organizations already have successful subscription offerings with multiple price points and wonder if they could improve with a free offer. It is always worthwhile to look at a broad range of options for providing additional (even free) value to subscribers and prospects alike.

But it doesn't always make sense to give the service away—even in a "lite" version. For example, in cases where there is no real interaction among users, such as accounting or security apps, there is no potential for viral marketing and network effects. So the only thing left would be using freemium as a means of gaining trial, with the potential to up-sell to a paid subscription. But in many cases, cost isn't the barrier to subscribing, as prospects are concerned about the efficacy of the subscription service.

And sometimes offering a free subscription for a mission-critical service can give the wrong idea—signaling low value. For example, if I offered you "free spinal surgery" and you had chronic back pain, would the "free" offer be enough to make you go under the knife? Most likely, you'd be more concerned about the quality of the surgeon, the likelihood of the procedure being successful, or the expected recovery than you would be about just getting a good deal.

When it comes to free trials and freemium offerings, another key question to ask is whether making some part of the service experience free is going to remove enough friction to engage new users. In many cases, the biggest source of friction is setup—changing habits, entering data, and figuring out how the solution works. Freemium requires enough value right now to keep people interested while simultaneously creating value for the business overall.

> Freemium requires a certain level of pricing elasticity, as well as a variety of upgrade options.

Freemium requires a certain level of pricing elasticity (that is, if the price goes down, consumption goes up), as well as a variety of upgrade options. If your service is not a luxury but a necessity and you already have a large installed base of people willing to pay for the primary service, you may not want to offer a stripped down version for free. This lite version might backfire and cannibalize your paid offering, or worse, it might not offer enough value to be seen as useful at all.

Don't despair if free isn't for your business. At the core, this "problem" is actually quite desirable. If people had already proven that they were willing to pay for the service, then developing a free service as a means of increasing trial might not make sense. In fact, it might be full of risk—cannibalization, resetting expectations, and offering users an experience that isn't up to your standards.

I suggest that you be creative in exploring free as a marketing tactic, but be open to the fact that your research may decisively remove "free" from the discussion. Too many companies are not disciplined in their use of free—and as a result find themselves without a viable source of revenue.

When Free Isn't Really Free: The Napster Story

It should go without saying (but doesn't always) that free doesn't make sense when sharing for free violates laws. Perhaps the most famous example is Napster.

Founded in June 1999 by Shawn Fanning and his uncle John Fanning in the midst of the Internet bubble, Napster was originally conceived of as an independent peer-to-peer file-sharing service that was known for free online music. Its technology allowed people to easily share their music with other members, bypassing the established market for songs.

The benefits for members were vast. They gained access to a tremendous library of music and videos while helping others—all without spending any money. It was the first experience millions of music lovers had with downloaded music and the opportunity to access new and rare single tracks without having to buy an entire album. And of course it was free!

Unfortunately, this approach led to massive copyright violations of music and film media as well as other intellectual property. Effectively, the free music was made possible by mass theft. Napster's original service was shut down by court order in July 2001. Later that year, Napster paid a $26 million settlement for past, unauthorized uses of music, as well as an advance against future licensing royalties of $10 million.[1] To pay those fees, Napster tried to convert its free service to a subscription system. But it had already "taught" its users not to pay for access to music. The company was acquired, first in 2002 by software company Roxio, and then in 2008 by retailer BestBuy, and then in 2011, merged into Rhapsody, the streaming media service. At the time of the BestBuy acquisition, Roxio claimed about 700,000 paying subscribers, down from a reported 25 million users at its high in around 2001.[2]

> Enlightened self-interest motivates tremendous sharing and cooperation and the creation of real value.

Napster's pioneering efforts paved the way both for peer-to-peer file-sharing sites such as Gnutella and Freenet as well as music subscription sites like Sky Songs, eMusic, and Spotify. But Napster was also responsible for slowing the transition of music to the digital world. Nearly a decade passed before paid digital music became mainstream. Ultimately, what Napster did well was to understand what the users really wanted and force the rest of the industry to deliver.

What can we learn from Napster about giving stuff away for free? With the right enabling platform, people's enlightened self-interest motivates tremendous sharing and cooperation and the creation of real value. The Membership Economy can lead to whole new ways of interacting with content and with people. Keep in mind, however, that:

- A business can't make money if no one is paying, even with 25 million users.
- Moving from free to paid for the same service is extremely difficult, regardless of the value.
- If you give stuff away, make sure it's yours to give away!

Remember

Silicon Valley is littered with failed companies that gave away any chance of success. While these companies are invariably shocked by their failure, this result wouldn't surprise anyone who has ever been warned that people won't buy the cow if they can get the milk for free.

There are lots of times when free does make sense—when users themselves, by using the service, create incremental benefits for future users; when the free users organically "touch" potential new subscribers and build awareness; and occasionally when trial is necessary to hook users on the service. Free membership in the role of "free trial" is most successful if there is a natural reason that certain users are likely to upgrade to a paid service—usually for increased volume, features, or service levels.

9

Use the Right Technology and Track the Right Data

If you had any question about how technology is penetrating our lives, consider the following statistics:

- Ninety-one percent of all adults have their mobile phone within arm's reach every hour of every day.
- There are 6.8 billion people on the planet, and 4 billion of them use a mobile phone. Only 3.5 billion of them use a toothbrush.
- Every minute, 100 hours of video are uploaded on YouTube by individual users.
- Ninety percent of text messages are read within three minutes of being delivered.
- The average 21-year-old has spent 5,000 hours playing video games; sent 250,000 emails, instant messages, and text messages; and has spent 10,000 hours on a mobile phone.

Traditional value propositions are being transformed by technology. This is not news. Look at what WebEx has done for meetings or BaseCamp for collaboration. Each has enabled remote collaboration at a different level than ever before. Both have contributed heavily to the "work at home" and "remote workforce/global team" concepts. With WebEx (or Google Hangouts) you can share documents, video chat with multiple people around the globe concurrently, send documents to the team, and more. BaseCamp is a web-based project management tool providing to-do lists, wiki-style web-based text documents, milestone management, file sharing, time tracking, and a messaging system.

What might be news is that there are dozens of apps, tools, and platforms that have been designed with the unique needs of the Membership Economy in mind. As with any organization operating in the second decade of the twenty-first century, technology is very much a part of every Membership Economy success story. In this chapter, I focus specifically on those emerging categories designed to support Membership Economy organizations that use subscriptions, communities, and networks as part of their business models.

Technology Matters—Especially in the Membership Economy

Technology isn't everything. It may be just 10 percent of what's needed to build a successful Membership Economy organization. The other 90 percent—attitude, marketing, understanding your customer, all of that—is critical, but the platform, apps, and tools you choose *do* matter.

Technology is the underlying major enabler of the entire transformational shift to membership. To paraphrase LinkedIn co-founder Allen Blue,[1] there's every reason to believe that the online systems are a shorter path to the same value provided by in-person relationships. Technology can speed up and simplify connections and idea sharing among members, but it also provides valuable insights regarding member needs and behaviors.

Membership organizations often are stymied by technical challenges, especially those that have been around a long time. The thought of change can be hard, and replacing or working around legacy systems can be intimidating. But there are lots of ways to leverage modern technology and execute on the promise of membership. Most Membership Economy organizations are not differentiated by their technology. They use services created by other companies to support their memberships. In many cases, they are accessing *software-as-a-service (SaaS)*, so the responsibility for maintenance, management, and configuration isn't even a principal challenge of the Membership Economy organization.

> *Nearly every kind of software is available on a subscription basis, providing flexibility, configuration, and affordability.*

SaaS options have made it both easy and affordable to build a strong platform for a Membership Economy business. Nearly every kind of software is available on a subscription basis, providing flexibility, configuration, and affordability.

Sometimes, the organization wants to build its own platform from scratch. After all, you don't want your key competitive differentiator (if that is the case) to come from someone else's products! But in-house development of proprietary systems is becoming increasingly rare. It used to be that IT departments would strive for big budgets and teams, but now, the most admired IT organizations know when to rely on other solutions for speed and reliability, and when to invest in building custom solutions. Using solutions created by others that are managed in the cloud can be great ways to manage costs and stay nimble.

There is a downside to the affordability and ease of all these offerings. Michael Geller, CEO of customer success software company Preact, pointed out that, "As a result of the declining costs to start a business, the cost to acquire new customers has gone through the roof, and retention has become more important than ever."[2] With all the noise in the marketplace, you really need to focus on retaining the customers you have. Technology is one of the key tools of the Membership Economy in part because it enables organizations to encourage and track retention in ways never before possible.

In any case, an organization that wants to leverage the power of the Membership Economy needs to consider its technology strategy as thoughtfully as it considers its operations, staffing, or services. Whether they develop custom solutions or work with vendors, organizations will be opening new channels or limiting connection with each decision.

Key Technologies of the Membership Economy

The technologies available to help you support Membership Economy organizations include social, engagement, loyalty, and billing. Here are some of the specific technologies you might want to bring aboard. It's not an exhaustive list, but it is meant to provide highlights of what's available:

- *Marketing automation (Marketo, Hubspot).* Allows organizations to track their interactions with prospective members during periods when they are not members (before they join or after they leave) as well as ongoing marketing over the member lifecycle. Important because sometimes it takes a long time to win a member and upgrade that member to the right tier of membership; and because sometimes even after a member leaves, he or she can be won back.
- *Customer relationship management (Act-On, Janrain, RightNow, Salesforce.com).* A system for managing a company's ongoing interactions with current and future customers, usually used in selling to businesses. Uses technology to organize, automate, and synchronize sales, marketing, customer service, and technical support. Often tightly integrated with marketing automation tools. Important because the balance of power has shifted from the organization to the member, which means that the organization needs to be continually delivering value to keep the member. There are hundreds of CRMs in the market today, many of which are customized for specific verticals—the options are endless.

- *Subscription billing (Vindicia, Zuora).* SaaS-based platforms that support nearly any kind of pricing model, no matter how complex. Important because they give organizations the freedom to design services that make sense for members.
- *Community (Jive, Lithium).* Allows organizations to provide a way for members to communicate with one another and with the organization online. Important because the more members can communicate with one another and with the organization, the more engaged they become and the more the organization can learn about its members.
- *Customer success (Gainsight, Preact, Totango).* Allows organizations to track leading indicators of customer health and drive deeper engagement. Important because members who don't engage and who don't understand the benefits available to them are more likely to leave.
- *Loyalty (Belly, Punchcard).* Allows organizations to track member behavior and provide recognition and rewards in exchange for loyalty. Important because it strengthens relationships, especially in retail, consumer products, and other historically transactional businesses.

Four of the most important categories to consider are billing, community, loyalty, and customer success. Some specific examples of providers of these functions are listed in the sidebar.

Concise Directory of Technology Categories with Examples
Marketing automation (Marketo, Hubspot, Act-On)
Customer relationship management (Salesforce, RightNow, Janrain, Optimizely)
Subscription billing (Zuora, Vindicia)
Community (Jive, Lithium)
Customer success (Gainsight, Preact, Frontleaf, Totango)
Loyalty (Belly, Punchcard)

Billing: Invest in Billing Systems to Support Membership Pricing

There have been many times when my clients have been limited in the type of pricing they can provide because of their billing systems. For example, one company wanted to provide a 10 percent discount to anyone who purchased two or more offerings. But because of the limitations of the billing system, the client had to create a separate product called "bundle" for each combination, thus creating clutter and confusion for members.

Two well-known providers that focus on billing for subscription businesses are Zuora and Vindicia, although there are many others. Both offer organizations the ability to offer custom, often complex, pricing solutions. These new SaaS billing services offer tremendous flexibility.

> Most subscription businesses suffer because they do not understand their costs.

Tien Tzuo, CEO of Zuora, points out, "When you move to the Membership Economy, you have much more flexibility with pricing and many more transactions (monthly, annually) which creates tremendous complexity—are you selling by volume? Duration? Services provided? Features available? The technology needs to support the strategic pricing decisions you make. You shouldn't be limited by your software in terms of how you price your offerings."[3]

A good billing solution can help an organization understand the actual cost of serving each member. Subscription billing expert David Werdiger, founder of the Australian firm Billing Bureau, believes that most subscription businesses suffer because they do not understand their costs and as a result are afraid to offer an "all you can eat" model because they don't know how much the average person actually will eat.[4] Fear that too many people will be heavy users prevents organizations from offering the pricing consumers really want.

Another often overlooked benefit of billing systems is the opportunity to use the billing communications as a marketing tool, providing relevant information about additional services in the invoices and communications themselves. Every communication from the organization should be seen as a potential opportunity to build brand loyalty and long-term connection—not just the materials that come out of the marketing department.

Community: Make Sure You Retain Control of Your Members, Even If It's Not Your Technology

Using an existing technology platform (like LinkedIn, Pinterest, or Facebook) can be a quick way to build the key functionality needed for membership community. It's fast and cheap and gives immediate access to your most loyal members. The risk is that the organization might lose control, the ability to offer something truly customized, and, sometimes, the ability to connect directly to members. For example, Facebook had a fan page idea, which a lot of organizations used as a means of building connections with their users. But unfortunately, Facebook recently decided to downplay the fan pages in its algorithm.

The result is that people who say they are fans of a business page, like Old Spice or Bare Essentials (two successful fan pages that have been developed nicely and with a lot of effort) are used to seeing updates much more frequently. These "reach" rates, which were at about 16 percent in March 2012, are now as low as 1 to 2 percent for brand fan pages, according to EdgeRank Checker, a tool for checking Facebook rankings, and are expected to drop to zero. Brands will have to pay for ads to reach their fans—even if those fans had previously indicated that they wanted to hear from the brand on Facebook. So now these brands that have invested heavily in building a fan base have to figure out a new way to reach this audience. Facebook wants them to sponsor their posts instead, paying for the privilege. Using a platform controlled by Membership Economy organizations like Jive or Lithium may be a better option if community is core to the business model.

Loyalty: Going Beyond Punch Cards, Retail, and Hospitality

Loyalty programs build ongoing relationships with transactional customers. The way they work is that the organizations track and reward desired behavior. A physical punch card is the most basic loyalty program—but there's a lot of friction in that approach, lots of ways that the customer can fail to gain the benefits and rewards of loyalty. They can lose the card or forget to bring it along. Even in the best of circumstances, a punch card can't track much in the way of behavior, beyond the number (or dollar value) of purchases.

> These new programs change the game for retailers and hospitality companies that have long used loyalty programs.

Today's loyalty technology companies can track much more. They can track every interaction that the customer has with the company, across channels and over time. Then they can build in analytics to create a picture of the customer's preferences and habits, and reward customers in ways that develop loyalty. These new programs change the game for retailers and hospitality companies that have long used loyalty programs. In addition, they enable a whole new category of organizations, such as consumer packaged goods companies and electronics manufacturers, to build direct relationships with end users—something that had been virtually impossible in the past.

Says Jamie Beckland, vice president at the technology company Janrain, "We are seeing that the types of organizations that are most interested in loyalty programs haven't done loyalty before—the consumer facing ones. What they're finding is that adding a loyalty experience helps them develop a direct relationship with their customer—which previously had been gated by the retailer."[5]

Customer Success: Track, Analyze, Act

It used to be that the relationship with the customer ended at the transaction, unless of course customers called with a problem. In those cases, a "customer support" professional would help them resolve the issue. Generally the organization would seek to minimize the number of calls customer support received. But in the Membership Economy, where customer engagement is critical, every opportunity to engage with the customer is an opportunity to build loyalty and long-term connection.

As a result, there is a new functional area in many Membership Economy companies, called "customer success," and there's supporting software for this too. Companies like Totango, Gainsight, Frontleaf, and Preact monitor and track member behavior—whether it's phone calls, emails, or actual membership usage—as a way to drive deeper value for customers. The more value or "success" members get from the offering, the more loyal they will become. In the Membership Economy, making sure that the member is successful directly drives revenue.

Implications for the CIO

What does all this mean for the leader of the technology team—the chief information officer? It means that with all the data being generated by the Membership Economy, the CIO at Membership Economy organizations has an opportunity to be a highly strategic player on the leadership team. Instead of being seen as the manager of a cost center or just a functional expert, the CIO now is on par with the CMO, sharing the opportunity and obligation to figure out how to collect and analyze the data that can drive decisions about what services to offer and which customers to focus on. Further, the CIO at a Membership Economy organization can and should be able to say to the CEO: "Here is what we should be doing to engage, retain, and even attract members."

Remember

Some people reading this book love technology and have embraced it in their personal and professional lives. For others, technology feels like a necessary evil, something difficult to manage and hard to justify.

Regardless of how you feel, the fact is that technological advancement is the single most important change driving the Membership Economy. If you remember nothing else from this book, I hope you take away the idea that technology can and should be used to build strong relationships with members. And even if you aren't a technologist yourself, you need to become literate enough in tech trends to have them serve you in achieving your membership objectives.

10

How to Retain Members (and When to Let Them Go)

My college roommate Elizabeth is a priest in the Episcopal Church. She posted a picture of herself on Facebook offering "Ashes to Go" to the faithful at the Arlington Heights train station, near Chicago, on Ash Wednesday 2014. How much easier can you make it for people to connect with their faith? Churches are increasingly providing extended hours for confession (or even offering confession online), child care, short and participatory family services, and prayer groups set up in specific neighborhoods.

Anything that adds to the effort required to engage with an organization reduces membership. This reality seems obvious, but many organizations require members to jump through needless hoops like filling out forms, meeting at inconvenient times or locations, or requiring complicated payment processes. The easier we can make it, the more likely we are to generate participation, which in turn generates loyalty.

Leaders in the Membership Economy know how to work membership into people's days.

Build in Loyalty from the Beginning

The best organizations start by building in loyalty from the moment a customer begins the sign-up process. They know that the first 30 days are the most important for building behaviors and habits. So when a member signs up for a trial or for a membership, it is helpful to optimize the member's initial interactions for success. Sometimes this concept is referred to as onboarding (discussed in Chapter 6, "Onboard Members for Success and Superusers"). You want the members to experience the breadth and depth of benefits as quickly as possible. Many organizations have special communication flows for new members in order to highlight key benefits or encourage members to get started in a simple but powerful way.

Increase Engagement Over Time

Sometimes, when members help others get up to speed, they become more loyal themselves. It may not be enough that they enjoy a personal or rewarding experience alone. Members often voluntarily improve the experience for their fellow members. This behavior should be encouraged, as it both works to increase the loyalty of the person creating the value as well as the members who benefit from it.

User groups have long worked on this principle of letting customers help one another. It builds relationships among members and also creates loyalty. In some cases, conferring prestige (title, status) on the most active users can further strengthen this virtuous cycle.

Another way to build engagement among members is to ask for advice or help. This technique works especially well with entrepreneurial organizations that are in growth mode, or troubled organizations trying to reposition themselves. Fund-raisers have long known that volunteers are more likely to make a donation than people who have never volunteered. People who give a little are more likely to give a lot later on. When people have given their time, their money often follows.

> Members need to feel connected to the organization and to one another.

Inviting members to create content is a way to engage them too. This is not a new idea—there have always been letters to the editor, for example. What is new is that technology is enabling direct posting and the fact that multiple media (video, photos, audio) are being used. These enabling technologies allow for increased creativity and often very professional results from amateurs.

Members, more than any other kind of customer, need to feel connected to the organization and to one another. Members can provide guidance and help to one another, can review products, and can even create new content for fellow members.

One successful campaign has been "Art of the Trench" (http://artofthetrench.com), which features Burberry customers wearing their coats in hip ways. Another great campaign by Disney (a leader in the Membership Economy) invites members to "Vine Your Disney Side" by creating a six-second looping video.[1]

Behavior-based triggers can remind members to participate more frequently and in new ways. Newsletters or tips and tricks that appear within an app can show members ways to get additional value without a large outpouring of energy, time, or resources.

Membership Economy organizations constantly reach out in order to understand what their members want from their membership. That's how the San Jose Museum of Art realized that its members wanted camps for children. It's how Netflix got the idea to expand into original TV series. Once they have loyal members, they figure out how to remove the friction that might cause these loyal members to leave. Table 10.1 lists the secrets the pros know in order to increase loyalty to a Membership Economy organization.

Make it easy	Don't screw up the payment process. Give value immediately. Ask for data only gradually. Devote attention to the onboarding process (most don't). Have a free option, to keep customers "in the family" even when they aren't spending money with you.
Make it personal	Periodically give them "something extra." Allow them to connect to you personally. Incorporate incremental setup to make switching costs feel high. Understand behaviors of loyal members.
Get others involved	Connect them to others via a network—create stickiness through relationships. Incorporate messages about how to engage with the organization and with other users into the product experience. Engage customers as sources of ideas, advice, and content.

Table 10.1 Secrets to Increase Loyalty: What the Pros Know

The "Forever Transaction": The Key to Loyalty in the Membership Economy

In some ways, the Membership Economy is like a marriage, with the expectation that members will remain loyal forever. But, just like marriages, that relationship takes work if you want it to last. Because the Membership Economy is about relationships and not transactions, the expectation is that both sides will grow and change over time, but continue to be loyal to the shared expectations.

> When good customers ask for small favors and you can give them, it builds loyalty.

The tactics may change, but the high-level benefits offered by the organization must stay true to the organization's mission. Membership Economy organizations seek a "forever transaction."

As in marriages, when the member feels that the organization isn't staying true to the brand promise, the separation can be bitter.

When you hear people talk about why they are no longer members of their gyms or why they deleted their Facebook accounts or why they switched loyalty programs from United Airlines to Virgin, there is usually a lot of emotion.

Certainly, there are "good" reasons for canceling a membership—when a person moves, retires, or achieves the goal that the membership promised (as in the case of dating sites). So not every separation is venomous. However, most memberships have no clear end point. Because there is no obvious spot to reconsider the membership—especially in cases of automated payments—when members reach the point where they are unhappy enough to cancel, they are usually genuinely unhappy.

A Few Specific Ways to Increase Loyalty

As I note in Chapter 6, onboarding done correctly dramatically reduces the number of people who sign up for trial or become full members and then cancel within the first month or two. It also increases the number of people who become long-term members. Members who participate heavily in the first few months of the membership are much more likely to renew than those who merely lurk. Ways to make it easy to be loyal include special incentives to longtime customers, removing all friction from any important transaction or activity members have to do, and making communication easy, for example, with a mobile app. Here are some specific ways to improve loyalty:

- *Build loyalty throughout the free trial.* While best practices say don't communicate too much during trial, the exception is if the person isn't utilizing the trial. In that case, you want to do two things. First, you want to send these individuals guidance to get the most out of the trial. A few days later, let them know you've noticed they weren't using the service and remind them to cancel before they are automatically billed. It's wise to remind them to cancel because otherwise you run the risk of their feeling tricked or, worse, refusing to pay.

- *Build loyalty through the acquisition phase.* If you're already tracking cohorts by lead source and utility, you may be learning things that can be applied in the acquisition phase. Every marketer knows that the sign-up process needs to be really simple and that you need to limit the number of options you offer. If you know that a particular cohort (say, coming from a particular key word landing page) is more likely to take Option 2, you create a sign-up flow that features Option 2 and its key benefits instead of focusing equally on all three options. While you can't have a separate sign-up flow for every segment, having a couple leading to the same offer can dramatically increase sign-up.
- *Build loyalty through simplification.* A lot of people think that initial acquisition is the end of the pricing process, but it's actually just the beginning. While you want to keep the sign-up flow as simple as possible, once someone has signed up, you can offer additional features based on use. For example, you can say, "For only $2 more you can get unlimited access." It's important to note that providing simple solutions targeted to specific groups of members often requires a lot of complexity on behalf of the organization. The simpler it is for members, the more complex it is for the organization to manage the options. In contrast, telecom companies tend to have complicated pricing, a lot of it confusing and feels unfair—which is why people are so frustrated and why T-Mobile stands out (we take an in-depth look at T-Mobile in Chapter 14). As Vindicia CEO Gene Hoffman once told me, "People on the telecom side underestimate the psychological cost of their complicated pricing model."
- *Build loyalty through personalization of the experience.* The definition of personal is "belonging or relating to a particular person." The best membership organizations allow for personalization of the experience.

One way to achieve personalization is to let people make the experience unique to them through configuration and customization. Another way to "make it personal" is to recognize the individual members. The Ritz-Carlton Hotel makes a point of calling customers by name, especially those enrolled in its membership program. Online communities nearly always use the member's name in the upper right corner and often "learn" from the member's behavior and use patterns, so they can offer a better experience—through product recommendations or relevant content.

> *You want your experience to adapt over time, and you want to continue to learn about your members in order to provide them with an increasingly personalized experience.*

There are three kinds of personalization—explicit, implicit, and hybrid. Explicit personalization requires members to choose what kind of personalization they want—a unique logo, address, or avatar, for example. Implicit personalization is when the organization learns about the member through member demographics and behavior and then adjusts the membership based on that information. Hybrids use both. Ideally, you want the experience to adapt over time and you want to continue to learn about your members in order to provide them with an increasingly personalized experience.

Marketo, an SaaS-based marketing automation software company headquartered in San Mateo, California, enables companies to create personalized connections with their members. It puts many of the practices it teaches into effect with its own customers. In addition to providing a full suite of marketing services, Marketo has established its own credentialing program, making it more like a professional association. It even tracks people after they've left a company and provides job boards to help them find other jobs.

Through user groups, big sophisticated user conferences, and a tagline of "the Marketing Nation," Marketo is starting to displace organizations like the American Marketing Association as the community with the most relevant people, ideas, and information for marketing professionals. Marketo Launchpoint is a community of additional services for marketers, should they not find everything they need through the Marketo tool. This attention to serving its customers' full set of needs, with a highly personalized solution, has built tremendous loyalty.

Watch Out for Passive Churn

Passive churn is when a subscription business loses members because of a problem with payments, rather than an actual decision by the member. For example, earlier I mentioned the situation in which a credit card on file expires and the member doesn't input the new expiration date—no fraud, but the algorithm cancels the person's account. You want to avoid this situation.

One of the biggest challenges many subscription businesses face is credit card problems that cause them to pause subscriptions, which in turn causes members to lapse or cancel. Often we cancel a credit card for good reason—to switch to a different card provider or to change a name in the case of marriage or as the result of fraudulent use of the card. At such times many companies give one or two email reminders and then cancel your subscription or put a hold on it. Once the membership has been stopped, there is friction.

This friction requires action on the part of the member—at which time the customer may reconsider the membership and cancel. Also, the friction itself can be annoying enough to make the customer cancel, or at least not update the credit card information.

To minimize such card friction, the organization should develop strong relationships with the credit card companies themselves (directly or through one of the many billing platforms optimized around subscription businesses) to see if a credit card issue appears to be fraud related or is simply a change in process.

The next step is giving good customers the benefit of the doubt when there is a credit card problem (which requires knowing who your best customers are) and reaching them on the phone to update the information while not suspending service in the interim. When good customers ask for small favors and you can grant them, it builds loyalty and minimizes attrition.

There are companies that optimize billing for subscription businesses, and this might be a wise investment, but there are also things you can do on the communication side to minimize loss. Gene Hoffman, CEO of Vindicia, one of the best of the digital billing companies, advises organizations to minimize communication relating to billing unless there's a major issue. He suggests that when organizations do need to talk about billing, they should make sure to be clear, direct, and generous when possible. The goal should always be to make it easy for the member to do whatever they're likely to want to do.[2]

For example, if your variable costs are low, why not give customers a grace period to update their credit card information? Send them a note telling them about the issue, telling them you're trying to solve the problem on your side and that you're giving them a grace period, but if they know there's an issue, to please update their account. Most companies just cancel or put a hold on the account, which can be upsetting to a good subscriber. No grace period also sends a message to members that they aren't really known or trusted.

The first time that the existing (already approved) card fails, you probably shouldn't say anything at all—wait until the second time, because most of the time it will work.

Active churn is the real issue—when a member decides to cancel. Minimizing active churn requires understanding the reasons someone might want to cancel. You want to make sure that you are attracting the right members in the first place. Then you want to make sure that they understand the value they're getting. Finally, ensure that they continue to receive value over time.

One good way to reduce active churn and maximize acquisition through the sign-up flow is by tracking data by cohort. This means analyzing the behavior of specific groups, and forming new processes to support them. Consider all three kinds of cohorts:

- *Date cohorts.* Measure elapsed time from the day they signed up to see if certain things happen after a certain fixed time. For example, dating site Match.com had a program in which it offered two months free at the three-month mark, which indicates that it was seeing a cliff at that point.
- *Utilization cohorts.* Do people tend to cancel after 10 days of low utilization? Maybe you should offer that group a proactive discount to keep them from canceling.

■ *Original lead source cohorts.* Do certain ads or partnerships bring in subscribers who behave differently from established members? If so, you may want to adjust your sign-up flows to appeal to the unique aspects of each group.

If People Really Want to Go, Let Them Go

People often wonder if "reducing friction" should extend to cancellations. There is some controversy about whether a membership organization should be like the "Hotel California"—where you can check out anytime you like but you can never leave. If members actually want to leave and intend to cancel their membership, it should be easy to opt out. Lots of marketers want to make it hard—for example, forcing members to call a number to cancel. However, the easier it is to leave, the more likely it is that a member will come back.

> There are specific types of engagement that make it hard for people to leave.

That said, it's important to build a system that makes leaving a difficult decision to make. Organizations often use the word "sticky" to describe such systems. People are more likely to perceive value in memberships that they use frequently and for extended durations, so many organizations faithfully track visits and lengths of visits of members as a proxy for loyalty and as a means of identifying members at risk of attrition.

Identifying new reasons to get members to use the service and incorporating use cases into members' daily routines make subscriptions stickier. There are specific types of engagement that make it harder for people to leave. For example, members are more reluctant to cancel memberships when they've achieved status (think airlines and hotels), customized their experience (once you've set up your online payroll system, scheduled your regular Tuesday lesson and Thursday tennis match), or built personal relationships (at church or the local health clinic).

Another way to keep members, although not always in the best interest of the organization, is grandfathering benefits or discounts into early memberships. For example, I stayed loyal to my phone provider for many years because I was grandfathered into an unlimited data plan (no longer, sadly).

When people still want to cancel, despite all the benefits of membership you have communicated to them, it is critical that the cancellation process be easy and clear. If it's not, they will complain to you and to anyone else who will listen about the onerous cancellation process. Complaints could have a negative impact on the company, but more importantly, making cancellation difficult is unethical. In fact, the people who process cancellations (and they should be people, not just an automated system) should be among your very best people—and ideally should have strong sales and customer service training. When people cancel, it's usually because they no longer perceive value commensurate with the cost.

In many cases, however, it can be because the member has had a bad experience that negates all perceived value, and the customer service person might be able to remedy the problem or apologize with a discount or gift. In addition, the person may not recognize the benefits that are available through the membership, and a conversation with a customer service person could result in a new recognition of resources. Many companies have early termination fees or discounts for long-term customers (two sides of the same coin) to provide members with an incentive for loyalty.

You may want to offer a saving ("Would you stay for half off?"). People worry that everyone will find out about the discount and ask for it, but data show that this doesn't happen much.[3] Everyone knows that you can call DirectTV and get a discount, but the offer changes week to week, and DirectTV is pretty sophisticated, considering credit history and subscriber length. If you have customers who are so price conscious that they are trolling coupon sites for a discount (and if they are otherwise profitable), you might want to give them the option. Plus it works great for retention. Price-conscious people are less likely to leave if they have negotiated a special deal.

If someone simply wants to stop paying, offering a free subscription—something that allows the member to remain part of the family—is a best practice. It allows you to stay in touch with the member, and you often can provide a more vibrant community for paying members (think of LinkedIn or professional associations). Making it easy to stay and logically hazy to leave is critical to the success of any membership organization.

When people cancel, do a quick survey to find out why. The survey is not so much to learn the problem (hopefully you already know the key reasons for attrition) but rather so that you know how to nurture them back into subscribing. Opt-out lists are extremely positively correlated. Because it was easy to leave, they know if they come back, it will be easy to leave again if they need to.

The survey should have just a few thoughtful questions that are linked to your nurturing campaign. For example, if customers opt out because school is out, you would want to put them into a nurturing cycle that invites them back in the fall. If they cancel because of a feature they want, you can let them know when you add that feature.

Remember

Membership Economy organizations depend on loyalty. And membership organizations have unique business model attributes that enable them to build loyalty into their offerings. Organizations like CrossFit and Salesforce.com have identified and incorporated numerous ways to strengthen the ties between themselves and their members, among their members, and beyond. They make it easy to sign up, make the experience personal, and get others involved.

SECTION III
MEMBERSHIP ORGANIZATIONS COME IN ALL SHAPES AND SIZES

In Section II, we talk about the different philosophies, strategies, and tools that make Membership Economy organizations successful. In this section, I focus on some real-world examples of organizations that thrive in the Membership Economy. You'll meet some of the pioneers of the Membership Economy, get an inside peek at their organizations, and get some insights into what they have done well. At the end of each chapter are takeaways.

I've divided this section into six chapters, each of which describes and illustrates a particular type of organization that is part of the Membership Economy:

1. Digital subscriptions
2. Online community models
3. Loyalty programs
4. Traditional Membership Economy companies
5. Small businesses and consultancies
6. Nonprofits, professional societies, and trade associations

While the categories have lots of overlap and don't include every type of organization in the Membership Economy, they can give you a good sense of the breadth and depth of this trend. At the end of each chapter is a summary of key learnings.

As I suggest in the Introduction, you can skip around and focus on the topics and organizations that seem most relevant to your unique situation. But I encourage you to explore others, even those that seem different from you, to see what they are doing to build membership.

Table III summarizes the key learnings you will find in this section.

	Why They Are Included	What Can We Learn from This Model?
Digital subscriptions	Customized pricing for value	Add higher-priced tiers to give subscribers options.
	Incorporating freemium	Differentiate tiers by service levels, features, and sometimes by usage volume.
	Building loyalty and flexibility into payment structure	Keep current subscription at same price.
		Raise the (monthly) price *only* for light users.
		Encourage users to commit to an annual rate.
		Pay special attention to billing systems.
		Be thoughtful about granting refunds.
		Innovate aggressively and continuously.
		Offer way more value than the subscribers expect.
		Identify early indicators of churn.
Online communities	Leveraging the wisdom and altruism of members	Provide immediate value to members even before the community is at critical mass to avoid chicken-egg problem.
	Freeing stored value in underutilized assets	Grow by clusters rather than scattershot to build connections.
	Using technology to build relationships	Make it easy for members to help one another.
		Make it easy for members to find help.
		Make it easy for members to express their ideas.
		Build in systems to manage renegades.
		Moderate the community to manage culture.
		Make small frequent feature changes rather than big upgrades.
Loyalty programs	Program members are 70 percent more likely to spread the word about your business (according to MarketingProfs .com)[1]	Can bridge the gap to bring transactional organizations into the Membership Economy.
		Create systems to track the behavior of specific consumers—move them from anonymous to known.
	Modifying behavior through tracking mechanisms	Determine what loyalty means at your organization—to you and to your customers.
		Provide benefits immediately to new members, even before they demonstrate loyalty.
		Make sure your members feel "known" by your frontline team—how would they be treated if they were actually friends of the frontline staff?
		Adjust and improve benefits as you analyze behavioral data.

(continued)

Table III The Many Varieties of Membership Economy Organizations

	Why They Are Included	What Can We Learn from This Model?
Traditional Membership Economy companies	How all the pieces of the Membership Economy fit together The timeless structure of the Membership Economy	Small tests lead to scalable solutions. Even if there's complexity in the back end, keep the user experience simple. Focus on the needs of members, and not on following the competition.
Small businesses and consultancies	Membership Economy potential without deep pockets How to customize for a local or highly specialized group How small can be beautiful, flexible, and personal	Keep focus narrow and clear. Use size to stay very close to members and their needs. Look for inexpensive, scrappy ways to achieve goals. Engage the local community.
Nonprofits, professional societies, and trade associations	Building mission-centric organizations Creating long-term relationships with members	Start with the organization's mission and evolve products and services to achieve that mission. Work collaboratively to achieve objectives with members at the center of everything. Engage the broader community in objectives. Develop sustainable strategies for the long term—fewer sprints, more marathons.

(continued)

Table III The Many Varieties of Membership Economy Organizations

11

What You Can Learn from Online Subscriptions

There is much to learn from the digital natives—the companies that were born online and that have integrated technology into their entire business model. Digital natives use the latest technology to support their businesses. They have tiered subscriptions. They tinker constantly to add features. They tend not to be flashy or do "big reveals," preferring to iterate constantly, changing the apps almost every day. Digital native organizations generally strive to design their services to be integrated into their members' daily routines—an ongoing relationship rather than a one-time event.

In the next two chapters, I focus on two types of digital natives, the ones that leverage subscriptions to provide access to content and services and the ones that build communities and social networks that bring people together online. Many organizations in the Membership Economy have blended these two models, but it's useful to look at each separately.

As I've suggested, everyone wants to crack the subscription code for loyalty and predictable revenue. Indeed, some executives think that

> Everyone wants to crack the subscription code. The challenge is that subscription models require discipline and consistency, tempered with constant tinkering.

a subscription business is automatically a membership organization. The challenge is that subscription models require discipline and consistency, tempered with constant tinkering.

SurveyMonkey, provider of web-based survey solutions, and Egnyte, provider of a single solution for storing, sharing, and backup of business files, are two examples of organizations that have built sophisticated subscription models to attract and retain loyal members.

SurveyMonkey: Going Upmarket While Staying True to Early Customers

The offices of SurveyMonkey, the world's leading online survey platform, are located in a brand new, four-story building directly across from the Palo Alto CalTrain station. The headquarters perfectly represent the SurveyMonkey brand, which has morphed significantly since the company's founding in 1999.

Current CEO Dave Goldberg took over the company in 2009, when co-founders Ryan and Chris Finley sold a majority share in the company to a group of growth equity investors. Goldberg's mandate was first to build the infrastructure to support the company's impressive viral growth, and second to leverage the company's position and profits to greatly expand the business. The 14-person team had built a profitable subscription business under the Finleys, with wildly loyal customers. These customers loved the quirky, friendly, helpful brand. Revenue in 2008 was over $20 million on a very simple business model: free for a pared down version; $20 a month (or $200 a year) for unlimited online surveys plus support.[1]

Subscribers saw the platform as a "secret weapon" that helped them make better, data-driven decisions and enabled them to be more productive in their jobs. Being the secret weapon for product marketers, human resource pros, and teachers everywhere, plus the fact that SurveyMonkey has always invested heavily in taking care of the customer, built incredible loyalty as well as positive word-of-mouth.

The Finleys designed the business model around access to the service, not ownership of the software, which was a brilliant early decision. According to current COO and CFO Tim Maly, "Since perceived value was always much higher than the actual cost of the service, and because it helped people succeed, and due to the fact that our support was top notch, the result was tremendous loyalty from the beginning."[2]

Goldberg's people needed to professionalize the already successful business and evolve it over time from a mere survey tool to the leading platform for helping people make decisions. Their vision included adding new offering tiers with even greater functionality, translating and localizing the product to make it more accessible to people around the world, and making the brand more sophisticated, while simultaneously keeping their loyal core and maintaining the brand equity that already existed. It's always tricky to change an organization's branding and core offering, but it's especially difficult in membership businesses because the relationship is based on ongoing trust and consistency.

SurveyMonkey was one of the first of the digital service companies (aka Software as a Service or SaaS) to embrace the freemium model, in which customers could choose from a free subscription or a paid, premium subscription with additional benefits. Maly talks about the initial selling approach as "consumerization of the enterprise." Individuals subscribed to SurveyMonkey and expensed the cost, which was negligible, to their organizations. Then they used the product so they'd be more successful in their decision making. Eventually, the CFO or CIO would notice that a lot of people across the organization were using the app and would begin to discuss a broader, perhaps companywide, arrangement. This consumerization of the enterprise approach has also been used by dozens of companies including Salesforce, Yammer, Box, and DropBox.

Over time, SurveyMonkey noticed that annual subscribers were more loyal customers than monthly payers. They were committed to the platform and used it in multiple ways.

Over time, SurveyMonkey noticed that annual subscribers were more loyal customers than were monthly payers. They were committed to the platform and used it in multiple ways. When members of the new leadership team came in, they wanted to rethink pricing to better serve long-term customers and also to make it easier for big organizations to manage multiple buyers. In other words, they focused on their best customers and optimized around them.

The new team incorporated multiple tiers, spending months carefully analyzing behavioral data about its current subscribers, looking at feature requests among different groups and exploring different ways to parse the new services that had been developed to please these groups. One key decision made was to leave the current option at the same price and offer significant new features and services at the higher tiers. The new team was careful not to raise existing prices, keeping the annual subscription at $200. But it did raise the monthly price to $24 (a 20 percent increase), figuring correctly that the increase would motivate the best monthly subscribers to move to the more economical annual price and that the customers they might lose would be the shorter-term subscribers anyway.

Then team members added two additional tiers, designed for more professional users, one at $300 and one at $800, or four times the original offer's price. While this seems like a big jump, it's important to remember that some of the companies using the $200 offering were sending hundreds of surveys to millions of users, so spending a few hundred dollars extra in exchange for more service and features was a great deal.

While some current subscribers upgraded, the vast majority of the subscribers at the higher tiers were new subscribers. SurveyMonkey's new offerings attracted more sophisticated users and generated more revenue as well.

SurveyMonkey has always invested heavily in product development, surveying customers, evaluating data, and conducting focus groups, all with the goal of understanding how people use surveys, what needs are adjacent to surveys, and how to deliver the highest-quality data. When I asked Maly why SurveyMonkey invests so much in innovation, even though subscriber satisfaction and retention are already very high, he pointed out that his company's mission around decision making is a huge opportunity. As long as demand is growing and opportunities exist to make it even easier for people to make great data-driven decisions, SurveyMonkey should continue to invest in innovation to exceed the expectations of both its new and existing subscribers.

In the past few years, SurveyMonkey has announced two major product innovations:

1. *SurveyMonkey Audience.* SurveyMonkey takes an anthropological approach to product management, watching how subscribers use the platform and then making it easier for them to do what they want to do. Product managers noticed that their subscribers often needed to find and pay for access to an outside panel of people to survey (usually matching specific demographic criteria), in cases where they don't have their own list. SurveyMonkey Audience took an approach that built on its unique strengths and met the specific needs of its members who require access to respondents for the surveys they design. The developers of SurveyMonkey Audience:

   - Sourced panel members from past survey responders.
   - Offered charitable donations as payment—not just to be altruistic, but because they found that survey responders who were directly paid for participation provided lower-quality data than those who didn't need a direct payment.
   - Limited the number of surveys any one person could complete to protect response integrity.
   - Incentivized customers to keep their surveys short to make them painless for respondents to complete.

2. *SurveyMonkey Enterprise.* SurveyMonkey has been moving toward the enterprise corporate market since Goldberg took over in 2009. Large organizations spend a lot of money to optimize decision making. Individual employees within 99 percent of the Fortune 500 have already found and used SurveyMonkey, so expanding

the services to meet the needs across the organization is a natural, often viral, extension of the platform. There are two phases to the strategy. First, the company strives to solve the pain points of corporate—legal, financial, and IT—and get all of the enterprise's users under a single umbrella. It has accomplished this phase with its initial offering. Second, it needs to enable user-to-user collaboration such as sharing of questions, surveys, and lists. According to Tim Maly, this is still under development but is expected to be available at the time of this book's release.

SurveyMonkey sees some ways in which subscribers are able to help one another; for example, by sharing aggregated data through shared surveys or by offering advice on making better decisions in certain vertical markets. It has noticed clusters of like-minded subscribers. For example, it has noted HR employees creating employee engagement surveys, teachers creating parent feedback surveys, and product marketers creating customer satisfaction and loyalty surveys. SurveyMonkey has created high-quality, professionally designed survey templates to meet these segments' needs, working with groups like the Society of Human Resource Managers and the Harvard Graduate School of Education. It has also enabled its users to easily share their survey results with others, typically colleagues or collaborators.

SurveyMonkey extends the community through its API strategy. An API, or application-programming interface, is a set of programming instructions and standards for accessing a web-based software application or web tool. A software company releases its API to the public so that other software developers can design products that are powered by its service. In SurveyMonkey's case, it has enabled people to connect SurveyMonkey to other related SaaS apps that they use (i.e., email marketing platforms, CRM apps, event management apps, etc.). It is also releasing a mobile software development kit (SDK) to allow third-party developers to build SurveyMonkey into their mobile apps. Through these strategies, it is bringing in developers as well as making it easier for subscribers to use the SurveyMonkey platform as part of their regular activities.

Enabling connections can be tricky because it has to be valuable for people to use and if not enough people use it, it's not valuable—a chicken-and-egg issue. Ironically, a great way to get a community started is by initially offering benefits that don't depend on community. In other words, users of SurveyMonkey, like users of LinkedIn and Weight-Watchers.com (see case studies coming up in Chapters 17 and 19, respectively), initially received value from the tools without needing to connect with peers. But over time, as the community grew, opportunities for user-generated content, peer-to-peer advice, and shared data added value to the membership. By allowing members more freedom to help one another, SurveyMonkey creates additional value.

In contrast, Egnyte, as a file-sharing service, has incorporated a viral component from its early days, and has leveraged partnerships with more traditional companies to build its subscription business.

Egnyte: Investing in Partnerships While Disrupting the Market

When I first met the young founders of Egnyte in 2007, Vineet Jain and Rajesh Ram were bootstrapping, consulting full time to support their families and fund their vision. Jain and Ram wanted to provide a hybrid storage, sharing, and collaboration solution for file management.[3] Unlike the existing cloud-only storage providers, Egnyte promised to support storage across a mix of local, private, and public clouds. This hybrid solution lets companies keep data on-premises or in the cloud, depending on how much security they need for each file. The idea was that they could provide a full solution for small businesses that struggled with storage and sharing of files and didn't have full-time IT teams.

> *Egnyte promised to support storage across a mix of local, private, and public clouds. Another major point of differentiation for Egnyte is its decision not to incorporate freemium into its model.*

Jain and Ram were really trying to transform the storage industry from an "either/or" solution—either you have all the security and control of a premise-based, owned solution, or you have the flexibility of a cloud solution—into an "and" situation where organizations could keep sensitive and regulated content in secure, company-owned servers while storing everything else in the cloud. As CEO Jain likes to say, "The cloud is not enough." This difference is just one of the things that makes Egnyte unique compared to much larger rivals like Box, Dropbox, and even Google Drive. And this difference was what attracted some of the most sophisticated investors in Silicon Valley, including Kleiner Perkins Caufield & Byers, Google Ventures, and Polaris Partners to invest more than $62 million in the company's first few years.

Another major point of differentiation for Egnyte is its decision not to incorporate freemium into its model. While Box and Dropbox have grown primarily through their free offerings and consumerization of the enterprise, Egnyte has focused primarily on serving businesses. It has a free trial to provide a taste of the value but has chosen not to carry free users in exchange for the buzz that freemium can create.

Instead, Egnyte is investing in partnerships with traditional "premise-based" storage providers. These partnerships appeal to the on-premise providers because it allows them to offer their customers the benefits of the cloud without requiring them to make a choice between the two options. As a result, these large companies, like Netgear, Synology, and NetApp, get to preserve their relationships with existing customers and keep selling storage boxes, while Egnyte gets introductions to large potential customers. It's a win/win.

As of May 2014, Egnyte had over 200 employees and 1.1 million users at 40,000 companies.[4] Customers go well beyond the small businesses that were initially targeted, to include leaders like Nasdaq, Home Depot, Ikea, and Coach.[5] The company sees blue skies ahead, as it continues to invest in partnerships, hoping for as much as 70 percent of revenue to eventually come from partners.

Says CEO Jain, "Egnyte has created a very successful business model by leveraging the Membership Economy. It goes far beyond just sales and recurring revenue. We have employed a customer success team to make sure both we, as a business, and our customers can continue to grow together. Our Membership Economy creates a mutually beneficial relationship rooted in trust, with shared aspirations of growth and success."[6]

For Egnyte, by harnessing its success to that of its members, it has built a model that creates ways for both sides to win.

What Can We Learn from These Models?

By building sophisticated subscription models to attract and retain loyal members, these digital natives enjoy predictable, growing revenue streams. In addition, they have planted seeds that grow across the enterprise. To attract members, organizations can use freemium (SurveyMonkey) or a free trial (Egnyte)—free options can really drive growth. We also have seen how organizations can add market segments as they grow. SurveyMonkey started with individuals and moved to the enterprise, while Egnyte started with small businesses and grew to bigger businesses and strategic partnerships.

Remember

- Add higher-priced tiers to give subscribers options. It is nearly impossible to raise the price of a current offering without backlash, but new and existing subscribers see higher-priced options with more benefits as positive.
- Use free only if it makes sense for your business model.
- Differentiate tiers by service levels and features, and not just by usage volume. SurveyMonkey enjoys viral growth in that survey responders often become subscribers. It is in the company's interest to send out as many surveys to as many good people as possible.
- Consider partnerships with other organizations in your space as a means to offer the full solution your customers really need.
- Try to keep current subscriptions at the same price. It is difficult to raise a subscription price without adding benefits.

- Encourage users to commit to an annual rate. While it is always good to test, many subscription organizations have found that moving to annual payments instead of monthly payments has a net positive effect on overall retention and revenues. Both SurveyMonkey and Egnyte have moved toward offering only annual pricing since their founding.

- Pay special attention to billing systems. Subscription businesses lose many subscribers each year because of avoidable payment issues—like changes in expiration dates or card numbers. In addition, offering all payment methods that subscribers like and being sensitive to local preferences make it easier for subscribers to pay and stay loyal.

- Innovate aggressively and continuously. While SurveyMonkey and Egnyte, like most companies, have financial targets to reach, within those constraints, the companies invest heavily in keeping the platform fresh, at all tiers, and monitoring customer satisfaction constantly.

- Offer more value than subscribers expect. When value far outweighs costs, subscribers become price-insensitive and very loyal.

- Identify early indicators of churn. Churn can be a lagging indicator of subscriber dissatisfaction, but there are ways to anticipate subscriber cancellations (like a survey!). Figure out what those are—they might include a dramatic decline in use or turning off the "auto-renew" feature. Have a plan for responding to these indicators to win back dissatisfied customers before it's too late.

12 | What You Can Learn from Online Community Models

Online community models might be the most radical of Membership Economy organizations. They are radical because there are no "products" as such. The product is the community and the content the community generates.

It's important to understand how tricky it is to start this kind of organization, to police it, and to cultivate its healthy growth. These community models use new frameworks to enable connection with the people we know, as well as to discover new people with shared interests who can add value to our lives. As Allen Blue, cofounder of LinkedIn and one of the true pioneers of online communities, says, "There's every reason to believe that the online communities offer a shorter path to the same value." [1]

Groundbreaking communities like Match.com, LinkedIn, and Pinterest can create real relationships and unlock stored value—information, insights, experiences—all provided by the members themselves. Their flexible peer-to-peer connections and the ability to create and share content and physical goods tap into value that hasn't been available before.

This value had been stored behind locked doors, in garages, and in the heads of individuals. These Membership Economy organizations extend the "infrastructure of trust."

As a species, humans have excelled at building infrastructures that extend trust and connection. I automatically trust my family. I trust people I've personally gotten to know well. I may trust one more layer of people, those who come with a strong reference from someone in my trusted circle. But without a legal, regulatory, and security infrastructure, I can't extend that trust much farther.

And without physical infrastructure—like roads and wires—I can't communicate with people and engage in trusting transactions even if I *do* trust them. If I move across the ocean from my family, for example, our trusting relationship isn't very useful if we can't communicate, transfer funds, or send packages.

With technology, our ability to communicate with a broader range of people gets better *and* our trust that these communications have some protections improves. As a result, it is possible to create trusting relationships today that we could never have had even 20 years ago.

In this chapter we look at how companies like Match.com, LinkedIn, Pinterest, and others are building new ways for people to engage with one another, how to provide the right amount of latitude when opening up new kinds of connection, and ways to harvest stored value. We also look at the opportunity that exists for many organizations to build communities among their existing subscribers. Membership Economy organizations go well beyond creating two-way communication between the organization and the members.

Match.com: Membership Is a Beautiful Thing

Match.com keeps its business fresh by constantly introducing and acquiring new models.

Match.com originally launched as a proof-of-concept for a company called Electric Classifieds which aimed to take newspaper classifieds online. For the "personals" industry vertical market, however, instead of using a traditional "pay by the ad" model, it launched with a membership model. The rest is history. With 2.38 million subscribers in North America in 2013 (an 11 percent increase from 2012), and reported revenue of more than $700 million, it claims to be "the world's first and largest dating company."[2]

Early in 1995, when the team was determining the business model, a key challenge was how to make Match.com a clean, well-lit place to meet people. The strategy was to attract women, with the belief that men would follow. At that time, team members were thinking about a ten-cents-per-email kind of model for people to contact one another, much like the 900-number personals and based on traditional newspaper models.

Match.com cofounder Fran Maier had just left her role as director of membership marketing at the venerable AAA motor club of Northern California when she joined the fledgling company. At the time, more than two-thirds of drivers had the AAA card in their wallet—very deep relationships and an extremely high renewal rate. Maier had become a big believer in membership. "Membership is one kind of annuity business and very powerful. It's just a beautiful thing. Look at those renewal numbers."[3] She believes that Match.com's decision to launch with a membership model has been key to the company's success.

Maier recalls saying to a room full of her (male) colleagues, "We've got to use the membership model. No woman wants to be nickeled and dimed." Her experience at AAA had taught her the benefits of membership. With a membership model, Match.com could provide exclusivity and become a destination for members, while being true to the brand promise of being safe, anonymous, and fun. For the company, membership meant recurring revenue, a model that was easy to implement, and the opportunity to build additional levels of service. However, the ability to take small payments was technologically challenging. While membership today is the de facto model for online dating sites, at the time, this decision was pioneering.

Retention is a tricky thing when the goal of the community is to get people to leave the community! The objective of most Match.com members was to find true love and cancel their membership. But Maier noticed something interesting that happened as a result of Match.com and the other online membership dating communities. They actually had a side benefit of making people more social in the physical world. Said Maier, "People started to date more, which meant they didn't have to settle for the people they already knew. People date a lot more now because of online dating. I think there's a lot less loneliness in the world, honestly." By extending trust through a membership model, Match.com has built a vibrant model and changed the way singles mingle.

Match.com keeps its business fresh by constantly introducing and acquiring new models. Acquisitions include People Media, which powers AOL Personals and operates such niche sites as BlackPeopleMeet.com and OurTime.com for older singles, as well as SinglesNet and OkCupid. It has also introduced new services for its core Match.com members such as Stir, announced in 2012, a service that hosts events like happy hours, cooking classes, and bowling nights for singles.

The Membership Economy relies on trust. It's about the consumer saying, "I'm going to stick with you, but I expect you to continue to deliver." It's the mutuality of the relationship that makes the model so beautiful. Continued innovation and evolution in support of delivering on that brand promise have been key to Match.com's success. Like LinkedIn, it has continued to expand its offerings over time.

LinkedIn: Using Freemium to Avoid the Chicken-and-Egg Problem

As of August 2014, LinkedIn, the professional networking site, had over 300 million users in over 200 countries and territories around the world.[4] Nine years earlier, LinkedIn had only about a half-million users. How does a new community grow like that at the same time that professional associations are lamenting declining membership and engagement among virtually all industry and functional associations?

The engine that drives LinkedIn's success is the freemium model. By welcoming everyone to use LinkedIn to store and share professional credentials and connect with the network, LinkedIn provides tremendous ongoing free value—a requirement for the freemium offer.

Even without the community and social network elements of the LinkedIn model, a critical mass of members found value from day one at LinkedIn, just in having an easy way to create a professional profile online. Over time, the network effect created by the broad participation of professionals increased the value of the community, as a means of keeping current status and contact information for one's network. It also made the premium memberships worth purchasing for a significant subset of members.

The vast majority of LinkedIn's existing network of professionals has never paid a thing for membership. However, it's the existence of this community that attracts the broad range of members. Certain groups of professionals—recruiters, marketers, and salespeople—needed additional services, and LinkedIn introduced tiered pricing and services to accommodate these needs. A subset of users upgraded to use the service more efficiently and to take advantage of the growing network.

> LinkedIn is designed to create a network effect. In other words, the more people who use LinkedIn, the more valuable LinkedIn becomes for the existing members.

LinkedIn is organically viral in that each member is motivated to invite his or her network, which makes freemium an especially effective marketing tool. As I note in Chapter 8, freemium makes sense when it generates three key benefits: viral marketing, the network effect, and up-selling. An important freemium criterion that many organizations don't get is that freemium must have real value; it can't be an empty shell that forces up-selling.

LinkedIn is designed to create a network effect. In other words, the more people who use LinkedIn, the more valuable LinkedIn becomes for the existing members. LinkedIn's leaders have given a lot of thought to providing significant value to the vast majority of members who pay nothing. They also think about what actions might justify a paid membership and have built in pay walls to prevent users from accessing that content without upgrading from free to premium status.

Joff Redfern, LinkedIn's vice president of mobile product, noted that the company called its users "members" from the early days, putting the member first more than most other organizations. Its leaders also spend considerable time thinking about the service's social system. He emphasized the membership culture that permeates LinkedIn's employees. "Our culture is members first," he said. "We are willing to trade off revenue for better membership experience."[5]

One example of this focus on the member experience happened with a recent product release. Code named Galene, the product launch represented the culmination of a year-long effort to scale LinkedIn's search engine and gather "all the economic data there is in the world—to obtain the world's first economic graph." Galene's design permits fewer search page views, which of course means less monetization for LinkedIn. But the team knew that the new design was better for the overall user experience. "Having such a strong member-oriented culture brings the right answer forward faster," said Redfern. "It's deeply ingrained in our culture and comes up all the time in product reviews, from informal chats to formal executive staff approvals."

LinkedIn is an example of leveraging one's core engine of free memberships to build a huge revenue-generating business. In this case, that revenue model created enough excitement to drive a market cap of $8.4 billion on the first day of public trading. The company projects 2014 revenue to be more than $2 billion.[6]

Pinterest: Driving a New Way to Search by the Power of Community

Pinterest is another digital native that has been able to unlock stored value by building an online community. While a newer entrant to the Membership Economy than Match.com and LinkedIn, it has quickly built a huge and engaged community.

Pinterest started as an online community with a social network component. Members can use Pinterest to "pin" content that matters to them. Pinterest makes it fun, easy, and visual to look for and find inspiration, ideas, and guidance on a virtually limitless range of topics. Members "pin" articles that they like onto themed "boards" that they create. These pins and boards are searchable, providing a fun and addictive way to explore content—anything from recipes to inspiration to travel ideas.

When Pinterest was launched in 2010, it was a community for people to share and discover inspirational ideas. It was a place for self-expression and the storage of relevant content for individuals. Initially, members had to be invited by an existing member or request an invitation from the company. Over time, it has become more of an open community, and today anyone can join. Businesses as well as individuals are joining, both pinning information and commenting on other people's pins. Bob Baxley, head of product design and research at Pinterest points out, "While it's tempting to think of Pinterest as just another social network, it's important to notice that Pinterest is also an online starting point for visual discovery, for search."[7]

Pinterest is fast becoming a key referral source for web traffic. For free social networks, this statistic is critical, because it demonstrates the network's advertising potential—and ultimately it's advertising revenue that sustains these companies.

At this point, Pinterest has accumulated so much data that observers are saying that Pinterest could rival Google as a starting point to discover almost anything that matters to humans, since humans are the ones doing the pinning that drives the searches. Because members not only pin stuff, they also tag it. As a result, the search experience is better than it is on some other search engines. Pinners use tagging words that make sense to them—providing valuable insight into how people think about the things that matter most to them. It's ideal to get recommendations from other people who share your point of view, and they're not necessarily people you are friends with. Pinterest is a network organized by interests, not preexisting relationships.

Pinterest is on the verge of transitioning from a quirky community that's nearly 70 percent female and mostly American, sharing recipes, inspirational quotes, and decorating tips to a formidable competitor to

Google as a more compelling, visual starting point for Internet searches.[8] The company has prioritized both global and gender expansion.

Pinterest is trying to figure out a better user experience—one that goes beyond community discovery and sharing and that becomes a true entry point for helping people find what they want. While Google has to rely on data alone to determine what might be important to a searcher, Pinterest is a database of what people care about.

Pinterest is fast becoming a key referral source for web traffic, behind only Facebook among social networks (although it's way behind—Facebook drives 67 percent of the traffic versus Pinterest's 10.4 percent).[9] For free social networks, this statistic is critical, because it demonstrates the network's advertising potential—and ultimately it's advertising revenue that sustains these companies.

The challenges in front of Pinterest include offering a cleaner introductory experience into Pinterest, making it engaging for men, and helping people find what they want to buy. Instead of going to Google to find an item for purchase, individuals would start with Pinterest, leveraging the wisdom of both the broader Pinterest community and the individual's personal social network. Pinterest wants to develop a long-term relationship with you over time because your interests change over time, and through the wisdom of the community, it can continue to feed your interests.

From a cultural perspective Pinterest is a mix of several well-known Membership Economy organizational structures. The founders came from Facebook, known for its hacker "just try it" culture, and Google, with its emphasis on big data and analytics. More recently, they have been hiring from Apple, incorporating expertise in design, as the organization works on creating a consumer-friendly user experience for discovery and search.

As Baxley, who joined from Apple, told me, "It's tempting to think of Pinterest as just another social network. But you have to think of Pinterest more like a search. If Google organizes by search query, Pinterest organizes by interest. And ultimately, that's more rewarding to the member."

It's fascinating to consider a membership-based search experience. Part of what makes a Pinterest search great is the visual element of all the photos, but part of it is the context of the network.

What We Can Learn from Online Community Models

At its core, the Membership Economy is about being known. By requiring a log-in, we can gather data about our members—and can create a much more personalized experience for members than we can for the anonymous guests. As LinkedIn's Joff Redfern says, "If we can identify you, we can personalize the service and create a better experience."

People want to be connected. They want to share and to engage with others, and the digital world is often a faster, more effective way to build relationships. A membership organization needs to till the soil, seed the ground, and protect the seedlings from predators, but most of the growth will happen through the community.

If you provide individuals with the infrastructure to enable them to connect and help them build behaviors that help themselves and others, there is tremendous potential to enable people to share ideas, content, and physical products that otherwise might go underutilized. However, as we saw in the Mixx example in Chapter 6, there are risks to providing too much freedom. There need to be safety valves in any community to protect individuals from poor behavior.

An online community can accelerate an organization's ability to achieve even the loftiest goals.

Remember

- Promote an ongoing two-way conversation between the organization and the members, and provide value through sharing among the members themselves.
- Build a relationship for the long term. Once you have a member, you want him or her to be with you forever.

- Unlock stored value through sharing supported by strong infrastructure.
- Understand that people's needs for belonging, friendship, and community can be met online, sometimes better than in the physical world.
- Support the real-life needs of communities with digital infrastructure.
- Be willing to evolve the benefits over time to deliver on the brand promise.

13

What You Can Learn from Loyalty Programs

An organization's most loyal customers disproportionately drive revenue and profitability. A 2013 article in *MarketingProfs* confirmed what most business leaders know:[1] The approximately 20 percent of customers who have visited a business 10 or more times drive 80 percent of the business's total revenue and 72 percent of total visits to the business. The most loyal customers are less price-sensitive, more likely to be up-sold, and much more (70 percent more) likely to talk up the business.

No one doubts it. Loyal customers are really important. After all, loyalty programs are everywhere. Our key rings and wallets are filled with plastic cards from supermarkets, gas stations, coffee shops, restaurants, office supply stores, airlines, hotels, and more. Most U.S. consumers (57 percent) join brand loyalty programs—both card-based and digital—to receive discounts on products and services, according to a recent report from TechnologyAdvice.[2]

A good loyalty program can bridge the gap between a transactional organization and a membership organization, modifying behavior, building loyalty, and increasing customer lifetime value. Such programs, when done properly, can be an easy and profitable starting point for transactional organizations to dip a toe into the Membership Economy.

The most basic loyalty program, a punch card, just tracks visits and purchases. When you amass a certain number of punches, you "earn" a free cookie, a medium coffee, or a discount. Many of today's loyalty programs are much more sophisticated. They generally track three primary categories of data:

- Demographics (age, gender, employment, income, region, etc.)
- Self-reported psychographics (preferences, attitudes, interests, etc.)
- Behavioral data (purchase frequency, types of purchase, revenue spend, response to marketing campaigns, etc.)

Caesars Entertainment, for example, might track how members engage with online offers, how frequently they visit various locations, what activities they engage in and for how long when they're on the properties, and how much money they spend. It also tracks self-reported preferences and demographic data.

All of these data are useful in painting a picture of each member, which can be applied to appeals, targeted offers, rewards, and products. To have strong, lasting relationships with people, it's critical to invest in really knowing them, and these data allow organizations to really get to know their members. Tracking behavior serves to provide a better experience for members and allows an organization to learn how members behave so that the organization can become more valuable to them.

I'm not a fan of most loyalty programs. While the organizations call participants "members," recognize them by name, and

Loyalty programs often feel more like a marketing tactic rather than a core element of a true Membership Economy business model.

have an ongoing, formal relationship with them (experienced as discounts in exchange for volume and frequency of participation), loyalty programs often feel more like a marketing tactic than a core element of a true Membership Economy business model.

The Membership Economy is more than a marketing strategy. It's about the whole organization being built around the ongoing customer relationship. There are some bright spots in the loyalty program world, however. Companies like Starbucks and Caesars Entertainment have truly differentiated themselves with their loyalty programs. And organizations like Punchcard and OpenTable provide a platform for smaller companies to provide loyalty programs too. All these organizations are using the data they collect and analyze to improve the benefits they provide to members and to make members feel more connected to the brand than nonmembers. That's what other organizations can learn. The tips here can help organizations step up their game with regard to their existing loyalty programs.

Loyalty programs are everywhere. At their best, they recognize the individuality of the most loyal customers and treat them as important parts of the whole, as true members. However, the vast majority of loyalty programs use a cookie cutter model that is not differentiated from those of their competitors. For many transactional organizations, loyalty programs have become a box to check rather than an opportunity to add a unique element to their business model.

We look at innovative elements in use by Starbucks, Caesars, and Punchcard, as well as some of the pitfalls United Airlines has encountered since the loyalty program it pioneered in 1979 has become a commodity.

Starbucks: Build Something Uniquely Tied to the Brand

"Whatever you do, don't play it safe," wrote Howard Schultz, the chairman and CEO of Starbucks Coffee, in his book *Pour Your Heart into It*.[3] "Don't do things the way they've always been done. Don't try to fit the system. If you do what's expected of you, you'll never accomplish more than others expect."

When Starbucks set out to create a loyalty program, it wanted to be sure that its loyalty strategy aligned with and extended its core foundational pillars:

- A great environment
- Consistent coffee and food across all stores worldwide
- Consistent experience

Ultimately, the goal of Starbucks is not just to sell coffee. It wants to build an amazing globally consistent experience, creating a "third place" beyond home and work where people spend lots of time. Starbucks wants to increase frequency in terms of visits and more engagement with the brand. Layering in the loyalty program is simply one more benefit to tie people in. Customers are already there and spending the money. By becoming members, they get more of what they care about—personalized offers, discounts, early access to products.

One really smart thing that Starbucks did was to use the wildly popular gift cards as a feeder for the loyalty program. It encourages all cardholders to register their card online. And by registering their gift card, they can begin taking advantage of the benefits of the loyalty program. Some people continue to use the gift cards, with their whimsical and changing artwork. Others (like me) have earned a personalized gold card by amassing 30 loyalty stars. In addition to looking cool, the gold card confers benefits, including free refills, free syrup, and periodic other freebies.

While the basic premise is the same as for most loyalty programs—give people benefits for volume and frequency of purchase—Starbucks has made some major advances on traditional loyalty programs.

- *The cards themselves are cool.* Starbucks has created hundreds of gift cards, and they are appealing in themselves. When you become a member and then a gold member, Starbucks sends you a plain gold card with your name embossed. They're really pretty and make you feel special. For someone like me who has a nickname that everyone uses, it's nice to have one place where people who don't know me still call me Robbie, not Roberta.

■ *The card is tied to payments.* Unlike the punch cards of old, Starbucks cards usually start as gift cards, which the member connects digitally to a personal account from the Starbucks website. The member can add money to the card, either electronically or at the register. Why is this important? First, because it removes a layer of friction, in that members only need their Starbucks card and not two cards or a card plus cash. Second, and more importantly, gift cards can serve as the gateway to membership, bringing in new users all the time. You don't even need your card to use your card. You can connect your card to your mobile phone through the Starbucks app, so it's even easier to pay.

■ *The card is easy to use* and has simple rewards. A lot of programs do some things well, but Starbucks consistently delivers on all of them. The rewards are generous and easy to redeem. Loyalty programs often fail because they are too complex. It's easy to get things wrong. Starbucks has kept it simple, removing friction and enabling positive experiences.

There's a lot of information to track, if you want to provide a good loyalty program experience. Companies need to track behavior, preferences, and status, and then, ideally, provide a customized experience that makes the member feel special. It's harder than it looks, and if the program doesn't work, members abandon the program quickly. The average U.S. household is active in eight or nine different loyalty programs.[4] So program structure, the redemption process, and refilling the card with value all have to be easy, and the benefits must seem worth the effort to the cardholder.

In contrast to Starbucks, Caesars has built a much more complex loyalty program, but one that has had astonishing results as it continues to grow and change in response to the needs of its members.

Caesars Entertainment: Put Members at the Center of Everything

Caesars Entertainment Corporation has used its TotalRewards program to build its casino business into a relationship-driven star of the Membership Economy. One of the first casino loyalty programs, TotalRewards was a huge hit when it was launched at Harrah's as Total Gold in 1997. The name was changed to TotalRewards after the merger of Caesars and Harrah's in 2005. David Frankland, principal analyst at Forrester, frequently cites Caesars TotalRewards as one of the industry's leading examples of how loyalty programs should be run.[5]

David Norton, CMO of Harrah's, came from American Express, an organization that knows a thing or two about loyalty (as we'll see in Chapter 14). He joined Harrah's in 1998, tasked with revamping relationships.

Caesars TotalRewards has been successful for numerous reasons, starting with the fact that the whole company is built around customer relationships. The company uses sophisticated data analytics and tracking to segment its members and makes its pricing, service design, customer experience, and operational decisions based on those data.

Management empowers frontline employees to become "local hosts" who use the data to make members' visits special.

In 2012, Caesars relaunched the program, doubling down with investments in technology, analytics, and employee training to support it.[6] The company tied employee reviews and bonuses to business metrics like lift, retention, and engagement, outcomes made possible in part because of the company's sophisticated technology infrastructure.

Within the first year of launching the new program in 2012, Caesars saw 20 percent growth in new members on a base of 40 million and a doubling of purchase volume at retail and dining establishments, achievements the company has attributed to the program.

Caesars sees itself not just as a gaming company, but as an entertainment company. It segments users to provide each group with a differentiated set of benefits and offers. It uses data to determine member preferences for things like favorite wines, room locations, and hotel amenities. Management empowers frontline employees to become "local hosts" who use the data to make members' visits special. This element is critically important because too many loyalty programs don't build relationships with members at all—they just provide discounts, thus encouraging people to join all programs across an industry just to collect the points.

What's important to note about Caesars' loyalty program is that it goes well beyond discounts to include local hosts and personal recognition. The company's size and sophistication has allowed it to build a highly customized program that really does offer a unique experience for the most loyal members.

Using Punchcard to Customize Membership-Type Relationships

Meanwhile, Punchcard, a Silicon Valley-based start-up, is building an online loyalty platform that allows consumers to collect points from any restaurant they visit, and allows individual restaurants and chains to customize offers for loyalty to build lasting

> A loyalty program that looks exactly like the programs of its competitors is not really a loyalty program at all.

relationships with their customers. Even small organizations have an opportunity to recognize their best customers and provide them with special benefits, access, and service.

Punchcard's website states that, "It is a local shopping app where you earn personalized rewards everywhere you shop. Simply shop at any local business, and when you're done with your transaction, take a photo of your receipt with the Punchcard app and start a punch card for that business. Add up the punches for that business and earn free rewards."

What makes Punchcard unique is that it provides the technology to enable specialized and differentiated loyalty offers through a platform for many programs. This is key because by making it easy for customers to discover, track, and redeem rewards through a single interface, it also makes it easy for even small retailers to participate in loyalty programs.

United Airlines and the Challenge of Commoditization

When United Airlines launched its frequent flyer program, it was a differentiator. Now, it's a commodity, and consumers expect it. While to some extent programs such as these encourage travelers to focus on just one or two carriers, travelers are not making the decision based on "best experience." Instead, they generally choose based on convenience of hubs and routes. The programs are expensive to run and do not differentiate one airline from another, so the airlines have become very cost-sensitive about the programs. This results in many of the most frequent travelers not liking the programs, even though they use them.

The airlines are an example of an electric fence rather than a magnet approach to loyalty. Even if you talk to people who have achieved some status (not the very highest levels where the experience is differentiated), they are likely to tell you that they don't really like their airlines and wish they had a better option. Not what you want your most loyal members to say!

What We Can Learn from These Loyalty Programs

Loyalty programs can be powerful, but need to be differentiated or they become box checkers and don't actually create value. There is room for a loyalty program to be a true Membership Economy program, but it requires constant innovation.

Remember

- Most members don't feel a sense of membership with their loyalty programs. While members like the benefits, many say that they see the loyalty program as a gimmick and not an authentic way of building membership.
- Real loyalty is more than a discount for ongoing purchases. Loyalty is about a feeling of strong support for someone or something, not free gifts for volume purchases.
- It is possible to be creative in a loyalty program. Look at Starbucks, Caesars Entertainment, and Punchcard.
- Data can be a competitive advantage, but you need to focus on personalizing the customer's experience and business metrics.
- Good things happen when you put the relationship at the center of everything.
- Members respond well to customized experiences and offers and to being recognized as individuals.
- Stay true to your brand promise.
- Empower frontline staff. Members want to be recognized.
- Remember that others will imitate you so it's important to keep innovating.

14 | What You Can Learn from Traditional Membership Economy Companies

There are companies that have been thinking creatively and aggressively about membership for a long time, even if they aren't digital at their core. I include them because these Membership Economy organizations led the way and have stood the test of time, often competing in crowded, sophisticated, highly competitive markets.

It's important to remember that membership is not a new idea, nor is it new for private-sector companies to benefit from membership models. They do some things extremely well—like building a strong brand and continuously reinventing services around the changing needs of members while staying true to the brand promise. But unlike companies using loyalty programs, the Membership Economy companies discussed in this chapter have fully embraced membership at their core.

We can learn from American Express and T-Mobile what mature Membership Economy businesses look like. We also will see how membership models can evolve gracefully when the organizations respond to the changing needs of their members.

American Express: Give Membership Its Privileges

Since 1958 when the company launched its first card, American Express and the idea of membership have been inextricably linked. Most American Express Card Members prefer to use their American Express card over others. They remember when they got their card and feel that it's a higher-status card than others. This illustrates the enduring love members have for membership models because they fill powerful human drives—like needs for affiliation and prestige.

Since the beginning, when American Express launched its first travel charge card and priced it higher than the Diner's Club card, it has always called customers "members," and has focused on providing special treatment for them. According to Elizabeth Crosta, Vice President, Public Affairs at American Express, the idea of membership, and service to its members, is core to everything it does. The company calls its members Card Members and not cardholders for a reason, Crosta explained, "Because they are a Member of American Express and that Membership gives our customers access to premium services unmatched by others in the industry."[1]

The way membership has manifested itself in the brand has changed over time. The "Membership Has Its Privileges" (MHIP) campaign actually ran from only 1986–1991, although people still use the line, which sometimes connotes a high-end focus that is no longer the case. While American Express has continued to provide premium tiers of membership, it focused on becoming a more inclusive and welcoming brand that provides superior service to a broader range of customers, dramatically expanding the initial vision of the card. This doesn't mean that it has changed who it approves for its cards. In fact, American Express is as prudent and responsible a lender as it has always been. Instead, it has created new products and services that appeal to new audiences that may not have thought American Express had a product for them. A great example of this is the launch of the Amex EveryDay Credit Card.

The Amex EveryDay Credit Card is focused on serving the needs of multitaskers—those balancing work and personal and family life—and there is no better example of a multitasker than a busy mother. While these customers would have been approved for an American Express card if they had applied, the members of this audience didn't think the company had a card that was right for them. They thought American Express was only for people who traveled frequently or who made large purchases. American Express spoke to these customers, learned what they wanted in a card, and created one to specifically meet their needs.

> *Loyalty is strong, but American Express needs to acquire new segments to grow and stay relevant as a brand.*

At American Express, membership has always been about something different: From the first day you get a card, you are a member. Membership delivers a larger community and a company that will protect you and help you when you are in need. Membership for cardholders is rooted in services. American Express is a *services* company, not just a financial services company. As it develops new products, it continually develops new ways to serve its members. Today, the company has products for travel, for shopping locally, for cash back, and for other benefits for people with a range of lifestyles and preferences. Its business has changed over the years, but it's always about putting customers first.

One of the biggest challenges American Express faces is how to communicate membership to someone who hasn't yet experienced it. Loyalty is strong, but American Express needs to acquire new market segments to grow and stay relevant as a brand.

Toward this end, it has invested in new membership experiences. For example, American Express is the founding sponsor of "Small Business Saturday." The day serves as the ceremonial kickoff to the holiday shopping season for small businesses, much like Black Friday is for larger national retailers. American Express launched the U.S.–based initiative in 2010 to help small businesses in the aftermath of the recent recession. Small business owners said that more than capital, they needed more customers to help rebuild their businesses. This program has since inspired a global movement with efforts in the United Kingdom, Canada, and Australia. Most importantly, this movement is much bigger than American Express and involves thousands of communities across the country, public officials like mayors and governors, as well as President Obama, who has shown his support by shopping with his children on Small Business Saturday. And, it gives American Express the opportunity to remind consumers about the important role that small businesses play in their local communities.

American Express is also investing in providing ongoing service and support to the underbanked—people who historically have not qualified for credit. It offers two products to attract this group to their community:

- *Serve* is a prepaid, reloadable card designed to provide an alternative banking solution to serve the 68 million underbanked in the United States. This segment has historically had to resort to payday loans and other economically disadvantageous options with high fees and low service. The card has a $1 monthly fee where permitted, which can be waived.
- *Bluebird* is a prepaid, reloadable account offered through Walmart. People can use Walmart cashiers as tellers and deposit money or withdraw it at the register. Bluebird members can write checks against the card as well. Bluebird charges a $2 fee for certain ATM transactions but does not have other fees common to prepaid cards.

American Express is an example of a membership brand that takes the formal ongoing commitment to all of its members seriously by continuously innovating and looking for new ways to serve.

Another giant company competing in a sophisticated, highly competitive market is T-Mobile. T-Mobile does not have the same long history as American Express, but it does play in a crowded, well-established market.

It's by differentiating itself from "business as usual" that T-Mobile has established itself as the most beloved of the often-vilified mobile carriers.

T-Mobile: Turn the Industry Upside Down

In 2011, value-priced carrier T-Mobile was testing pricing on data plans for tablet devices. Management already knew that its customers hated to be locked in by a contract, and, in fact, T-Mobile had been among the first of the carriers to offer month-to-month contracts. Managers knew they needed a program that would appeal to three key groups:

- "Connected Family" (just like it sounds—families)
- "Social Communicators" (20-somethings who use phones primarily for social purposes)
- "Aspiring Tech Enthusiasts" (people in their 20s and 30s who love gadgets but can't afford them so they are later adopters than they would like to be)

Was there a way to simplify pricing to appeal to these groups? While crafting a brand positioning strategy for T-Mobile Broadband, Lindsay Pedersen of LCP Consulting interviewed people to determine directionally how people wanted to pay and how much data they wanted.

What she found was surprising. All of the 60 people she interviewed said they preferred an "all you can eat" package. On its surface, this behavior seems completely irrational. Yet, like the all-you-can-eat buffets in Las Vegas, T-Mobile consumers prefer the benefits of access, freedom from risk, and perceived bargain over the actual value of paying (less) for what they are likely to consume.

Pedersen recalls, "The resulting positioning I recommended—and that's used to this day for T-Mobile Broadband—is 'Freedom to connect richly from anywhere.' Or, as the copywriters put it, 'Take the Internet where life takes you.' It was about freedom."[2] For T-Mobile, this was an early step in what has become one of the most impressive turnarounds in recent history.

Today T-Mobile is transforming the wireless industry with its "uncarrier strategy." It is removing the shackles of required loyalty—the dreaded two-year cell phone contract. In so doing, they are unleashing the kind of voluntary loyalty they believe will result in a true "forever transaction."

> Today we look at T-Mobile's decision to end contracts as a brilliant win, but at the time it was seen as a "betting the farm" kind of move that paid off.

This transformation started from the top, with the bold leadership of a new CEO, John Legere. When you think of wireless companies today and the advanced technology, it's easy to forget that they grew out of archaic public utilities. It was from giant, monopolistic dinosaurs that the wireless companies learned how to treat their customers. All the major carriers knew their customers hated contracts, but T-Mobile was in a dire situation when Legere took over, and the board gave him the freedom to take some big risks.

Legere challenged his team members to think of themselves as the target customer.

I talked to Iniko Basilio, a T-Mobile marketing director, about what drove the pivot. He told me he thinks that the company moved its focus away from responding to competitors. Instead, it went back to basics and focused on its own customers. What was bothering them? "If you were an alien who arrived to earth, what would you think about the way the U.S. wireless industry treats customers?"[3]

T-Mobile's offering did not align with its mission: "To help our customers build richer relationships and networks with the people and things that matter to them most." Why require two-year contracts with each new device when customers wanted to upgrade hardware more frequently? Why force consumers to buy a subsidized phone and stick with it if they wanted a new one in six months? Then the marketing organization championed a really radical question: What if we get rid of contracts and don't lock customers into one? After all, if customers are unhappy, they'll find a way to leave you no matter what!

At the same time that T-Mobile abolished contracts it simplified the wireless shopping experience. When a customer walked into a T-Mobile retail store, there were too many options and pricing permutations. The complexity was creating friction and turning choosing into work. So the company made pricing simple: unlimited talk and text on all plans with the only difference based on what matters most to customers—the amount of high-speed data they needed.

Then T-Mobile got really creative. It turned its model upside down to make its members love the company. Employees were given the latitude to make the changes needed to truly delight members. Basilio remembers this time as very liberating for the employees, because they could finally focus on creating long-term relationships with customers, instead of constantly asking, "OMG, what's Verizon doing? Let's respond to that."

These external changes in the member-company relationship are mirrored inside the company. T-Mobile embraces a model called "team together, team apart." The idea is that you can debate something furiously within your team, and then align completely once the group makes a decision. Once you make a decision beyond your own department, you become a team together instead of a team apart.

Basilio concedes to the occasional "soul-crushing moments of disempowerment" because employees are so passionate and believe they have the best solution. But most of the time, he feels that the emphasis across the organization is to identify the pain points that matter most to customers and then address them with relevant solutions. It's the ideal environment for a customer-centric marketer. What he loves about the culture is a focus on the right thing, members, and the fact that people from leadership on down are passionate about understanding the pain points of their members. "We're not finding a cure for cancer, but we are humbly making an impact on something that matters to our customers. Their problems are our problems."

> Sometimes the most successful strategies are not best from a short-term business case perspective.

Not everything has changed at T-Mobile. It's still data-driven and analytical. It still does a lot of white-boarding—standing around a white board and charting goals and processes. But now it's swinging for the cheap seats instead of hoping for a walk. Sometimes the most successful strategies are not best from a short-term business case perspective. Throughout the organization, now people are encouraged to take calculated risks and think about the big picture.

Different mobile customers have very different needs. Small business owners, families, people who just need a single line, gamers, travelers—the mobile phone carriers have hundreds of niche markets to reach. So carriers get knocked for not being responsive, even though they are highly fractured. Most carriers have focused on acquisition using a simple if commoditized message: price. Retention therefore becomes much, much harder—since without focus on attracting the right customers, the acquisition funnel can become more of a sieve.

T-Mobile tries to show its customers, from the moment of initial contact throughout the onboarding process, that the company is different. The company has implemented an outbound calling program in which the person who sold the service follows up with a phone call two weeks after the initial transaction. These calls don't seem to bother customers, but they often lead to an additional visit to the store—either to set up a feature, troubleshoot, or even buy additional accessories or insurance. Not only is the customer happier since T-Mobile implemented the follow-up calls, but there is measurable revenue resulting from this postsale dialogue. The store has become a point for strengthening relationships beyond the initial transaction, and the employees have become customer success agents rather than order takers.

T-Mobile has over 50 million customers, but is still smaller than its three competitors.[4] The mobile carrier business is saturated, big, and highly competitive. There's hardly anyone over the age of 10 in the United States who doesn't have a mobile phone. Effectively, the companies are only competing for each others' churn by providing increasingly better experiences for specific market segments. T-Mobile eliminated contracts, yet its churn is decreasing. It has chosen to build a magnet instead of an electric fence, and the company is winning. Members are choosing to stay because of the experience, loyally paying their monthly subscription fees, even without a contract.

What We Can Learn from Traditional Membership Economy Companies

What must big corporations do to stay strong in the Membership Economy? They need to focus on the members—their needs, their frustrations, their satisfaction—rather than on corporate bureaucratic rules or competition. They need a clear brand promise versus "me too." They need to have their members' backs, like American Express. They need to focus on what members really want and be willing to take a different path from the competition, as T-Mobile did. By staying close to their members, both American Express and T-Mobile have continued to evolve their offerings, staying relevant and differentiating themselves from their formidable competition.

In the preceding chapter we considered loyalty programs through the examples of companies like Starbucks, United Airlines, and Caesars Entertainment. These companies have certain traits in common with blue-chip traditional Membership Economy companies like those profiled in this chapter. Both types of companies are competing in highly sophisticated, crowded markets. Both use data to really understand their customers, and they offer a deceptively simple value proposition, backed up by a lot of customization. A difference in their strategic response that leaps out at me is that the loyalty program companies haven't really embraced membership—they've siloed it. Unlike the blue chips we discuss, they haven't put the member relationship at the center of everything. They may be creating loyalty, but they are not creating the conditions for their customers to feel a true sense of membership.

Remember

- Even as the mission stays constant, the delivery needs to change.
- Keep measuring results and asking members for feedback.
- As you develop new products, be sure that you understand how they will serve members.
- Consider and invest in new membership experiences.
- Respond to member needs and concerns, not superficial competitive moves.
- Simplify pricing, especially at the moment of conversion.
- Make the members' problems the organization's problems—and then solve them.

15 | What You Can Learn from Small Businesses and Consultancies

Membership Economy communities don't have to be big to be effective. In fact, being small can be a competitive advantage because a small organization can focus on serving the ongoing, changing needs of a specific audience. In most cases, the entrepreneur can access off-the-shelf technology cheaply. There are dozens of SaaS-based software tools designed to support small businesses. Technology to drive operations is not the primary cost in a small business; usually the greater cost is in defining the model, developing the content, and managing the community.

In this chapter, we look at different kinds of small businesses to prove that nearly any type of business can be a membership organization. We'll see how two relatively small organizations have successfully harnessed the power of membership to build community, unlock stored value, and generate predictable revenue.

How Mom and Pop Can Embrace the Membership Economy

I love getting my nails done. It's something I share with my two teenage daughters. They choose my colors, and we discuss *People* magazine articles. It's a great way to relax and spend time with my teenagers.

Most nail salons have peak hours. This means that they also have trough hours, when the salon is empty and the technicians end up hanging out in the back killing time.

Imagine a new "Membership Economy Salon." Members pay a monthly fee for a full manicure every month, with unlimited polish changes during off hours. Regular monthly manicures are at fixed times, so subscribers get to know the others in their time slot and build relationships. Instagram and Facebook accounts feature cool new colors and trends in nail design. And members can pay extra to come to seasonal "members only" nights for cocktails and pampering. Such a solution exists in Westchester, New York, at The Nail Concierge, a spa treatment business that rewards customers for becoming members, including extra treatments, gifts, and discounts. Possibilities for the Membership Economy are limitless.

Technology's most recent changes should disproportionally benefit the smallest of businesses. Look at Yelp, a hyper-local Membership Economy company that builds on trusted reviews of small businesses. And companies like Foursquare that make it easy to track loyalty to specific restaurants. Big channels like Twitter, Pinterest, and Facebook can further build community and familiarity, turning patrons into members who know each other.

As I've already mentioned, loyalty programs can dramatically improve retention and lifetime customer value—and even small businesses can implement these programs. In addition, community platforms and online services have made it affordable and relatively easy to extend the engagement between members and their service providers between face-to-face meetings, as well as to build relationships among members. The Membership Economy isn't just for the big guys.

Capitalize on the personal connection that is difficult for big companies to establish.

The secret here is the combination of online and offline channels—leveraging online to touch members more frequently and to enable flexible scheduling of live events. Think about the ongoing value you can provide to your members and what would make them feel special and connected. Develop pricing that rewards your most loyal customers and increases their use of your facilities. And capitalize on the personal connection that is difficult for big companies to establish.

Kepler's Books: The Retailer Rescued by the Membership Economy

When a Menlo Park bookstore was economically threatened, the community stepped in and created a membership program to improve long-term sustainability.

Founded in 1955 by peace activist Roy Kepler, Kepler's Books is a large independent bookstore. After its founding, it quickly became a center for intellectual thought and community discussion for the people living in the suburbs surrounding Stanford University. Over the years, the bookstore moved to increasingly larger locations, until it found its current home in downtown Menlo Park, California. Kepler's is a neighbor to many of the Membership Economy pioneers featured in this book. After its move to Silicon Valley, many of the most innovative and successful investors and entrepreneurs frequented Kepler's as a favorite browsing destination.

By 2005, however, the bookselling landscape had changed, due in large part to the innovations of online retailers like Amazon. On August 31, 2005, Kepler's Books closed its doors.

What happened next at Kepler's was unprecedented and a great example of the Membership Economy in action. Local citizens responded with demonstrations to support Kepler's and to protest the loss of their favorite bookstore. Citizens including Ricky Opaterny, an early Google employee and a Kepler's fan, and serial entrepreneur and local resident Daniel Mendez and his wife Vivian Leal organized supporters to restructure Kepler's and raise new capital. Within weeks,

Kepler's reopened its doors with new shareholders from the community, a renegotiated lease, a new board of directors, a new Literary Circle Membership Program, and tons of volunteer support.

Over the next few years the membership program provided funds to expand Kepler's events programming and community activities leading it to win many awards and industry recognition. In 2012, Kepler's was taken over by Praveen Madan and his wife Christin. Madan has said he wants to turn Kepler's into a member-owned business such as outdoor clothing and gear store REI or the publicly owned Green Bay Packers football team.[1]

Their current plan, supported by community members, is known as Kepler's 2020. Under this innovative plan Kepler's award-winning events program was transferred into a new nonprofit organization with a vision of growth and sustainability. The new nonprofit called Peninsula Arts & Letters was able to get off the ground by raising start-up capital from the community, including many Literary Circle members.

Today, Kepler's Books has become a role model for independent bookstores from all over the world, many of whom are turning to their communities for more formal support in competing against the online retailers and major chains. While Clark Kepler is no longer the owner of Kepler's, he advises companies on improving their community focus and participating in the Membership Economy. While the Membership Economy isn't for all small businesses, he notes that it can provide a useful model for organizations that have already developed strong loyalty. He told me, "Certainly membership models represent one future for small businesses, however, they must be authentic and community-focused to warrant customer loyalty."

Examples of Small-Business Loyalty Programs
Independent bookstore: Kepler's, http://www.keplers.com. Looked to its community for funding and support to stay open and independent, transitioning to a membership model with an outside board of directors to subsidize the community-oriented programming.

> *Hotdog purveyor:* Devil Dawgs, http://devildawgs.com. Uses technology provided by Belly to create a customized loyalty program that rewards customers with free food, drinks, and even the right to name a hotdog.
>
> *Nail salon:* The Nail Concierge, http://thenailconcierge .com. Offers memberships to regular customers, including confirmed appointments, discounts, and extra treatments.

Kepler's has gone beyond the typical loyalty program that many retailers use and built membership into its whole model. But small businesses beyond retailers can leverage membership through focus on their unique value. Many independent consultants have been able to build communities around the intellectual property they've created and the clients they've already attracted. One very successful example is Alan Weiss.

Alan Weiss: The Consultant with the Million-Dollar Community

Million Dollar Consultant Alan Weiss often says that he tries to be done with his workday by 2 p.m. so he can spend the rest of his day by the pool. The self-titled "Architect of Communities" has built a vibrant community of independent consultants and is earning millions, much of it thanks to the power of the online and real-world community he has built. Thousands of consultants attribute their success to Weiss's thought leadership and community.

Most consultants first learn about Weiss through one of his many books[2] and then find their way to his website, where they can sign up for any number of newsletters, free and paid. The website also has lots of free content.[3] That's how I first met Weiss, who has been my mentor for many years.

> *Weiss creates new intellectual property constantly. His expertise is still the primary draw, but, increasingly, members are finding tremendous value from the other members.*

Typically, many sign up for a $3,500-plus, six-month mentoring experience, delivered by one of the mentors personally trained by Weiss. Weiss pays the mentors, deducting a one-time fee. There are many other programs, ranging in price from $1,000 for a half-day session with Weiss to $15,000 and up for weeklong programs. Participation in these programs grants consultants membership in Weiss's community. It also gives them access to certain free services forever, including the live two-day events called Mentor Summits, Weiss's active online forums, and periodic teleconferences. Over time, Weiss has to do less and less while the network effect of the strong and engaged community builds more and more value for the members.

The community has freed up considerable time for Weiss and created a passive revenue stream. Simultaneously, Weiss is empowering members of his community to educate others and benefit financially. It's a win-win-win for the Master Mentors, for the consultants, and for Weiss too, who can focus on creating new services for his members.

Members are fiercely loyal to Weiss and to the community and participate actively and generously. Weiss creates new intellectual property constantly. His expertise is still the primary draw, but, increasingly, members are finding tremendous value from the other members. Recently, Weiss has added higher-level, more expensive offerings, including a coaching program called "Kick Ass and Take Names" and membership cards which provide big discounts and extra benefits for committing to a certain level of annual participation in the community.

A key part of Weiss's value has become access to the membership community he has built. Weiss has built structures to enable communication and support across the community—and the development of strong relationships among members. Master Mentors volunteer at annual meetings to provide free workshops, and a culture of mutual support adds value to all members, regardless of how much they pay. By engaging his community, Weiss has both extended the reach of his intellectual property and freed up his time to develop more ways to deliver value to his members.

Examples of Thought-Leader Membership Economy Communities

- *Alan Weiss:* http://www.alansforums.com. Online community for independent consultants, with both free and paid opportunities, including access to live educational experiences, online webinars, recorded and written content, and online forums.
- *Dave Ramsey:* http://www.daveramsey.com/home/. Financial advice for individuals across a range of topics, with both free and paid opportunities, including access to live educational experiences, online tools, classroom curricula, videos, books, and webinars.
- *Michael Hyatt:* https://platformuniversity.com/members/onhold/. Marketing and public relations expertise delivered via monthly subscription. Features include master classes, forum access, live Q&A, and recorded/written content.

What You Can Learn from Small Businesses and Consultancies

You don't need to be big to leverage the power of the Membership Economy. Independent retailers like Kepler's can use membership to rally their community and ensure their ongoing stability. As you'll see in the next chapter, a single, determined entrepreneur can build a professional association supporting hundreds of business owners without raising outside capital. And thought leaders can use membership to extend the reach of their ideas well beyond their clients and speaking venues. The important thing is to take time to determine the value you provide your members and to build additional membership around those needs.

You have seen several small businesses and firms that are leveraging the Membership Economy to generate value for their members.

They have proven that they don't need a lot of resources to extend their reach and impact by building ongoing relationships. If they can do it, anyone can do it.

Remember

- Focus on your best clients as you build your membership organization, and create valuable experiences that would attract like-minded people.
- Turn your processes into products and license them. Create worksheets, lesson plans, and reading materials that will let other "trainers" educate your audience on your content.
- Consider an in-person event once you have critical mass in a particular region. This could be a breakfast with a guest speaker or an all-day event.
- Consider building your membership around an "institute" you build—an institute, after all, is simply a research organization. Or a lab—testing things is good too. People crave the certainty of validated methodologies.
- Aim toward achieving a big mission. How is the world going to be better because you have been here?
- Enable your best members to teach one another your content. Bring them together to talk about what you do so well and how others can do it. By teaching others, they get better, and you have to work less—it's a virtuous cycle!
- Offer advisory circles for small groups of members in which they meet privately and in groups with your oversight—a great way to build direct relationships and value while also forging strong communities.
- Offer regular (monthly) webinars and invite everyone in your free community. Charge a small price. Record the webinars and make them available for future subscribers to your webinar series.

- Create a free, online community. Offer loads of free or inexpensive content to your online community. This could be white papers, e-books, podcasts, or videos. It could be interviews or musings or how-tos.
- Constantly invest in expanding your free community by writing, speaking, and emailing (including sending emails to lists that you buy or share).

16

What You Can Learn from Nonprofits, Professional Societies, and Trade Associations

Professional associations, environmental groups, museums, and other nonprofits have been in the Membership Economy longer than anyone. They tend to see themselves as being different from profit-making enterprises. While they do have some major differences, they are more like private sector membership organizations than they think. And they have a lot to teach other Membership Economy organizations.

Like private sector companies, nonprofits seek to provide ongoing value for their members. However, they have some unique challenges. They are committed to a nonchanging mission, which sometimes requires them to make financially disadvantageous decisions. Nonprofits and associations often have cumbersome governance models. Their goals can be hard to measure. Today, the missions of many nonprofits are being eaten away by private sector companies that are providing targeted and profitable benefits. These up-starts are disrupting the normally methodical, collaborative, and slow-moving associations. While nonprofits have clear missions, strong visions, and membership-oriented cultures, they need to constantly reinvent themselves in order to stay fresh.

Paul Shoemaker, the founder of Social Venture Partners International, thinks the biggest challenge for nonprofit impact is scalability. He points out that nonprofits don't have access to capital for massive growth the way the private sector does. As a result, they need to be scrappy and work collaboratively both inside the organization and with other nonprofits. This idea of collaborating with other nonprofits with overlapping missions has become quite trendy and is known as "collective impact."

Nonprofits and associations face challenges that are common across the Membership Economy, changing how they deliver on their mission while staying true to their promise. Most of the ones that have been around the longest have had to figure out how to manage the lifecycle of programs and processes that become obsolete.

In this chapter we look at APPO (the Association of Personal Photo Organizers), an interesting, relatively new professional association, and the Sierra Club, a large, mature advocacy group. We'll see what they have in common, what they know about building loyalty, and how they handle the unique challenges that come with their respective sizes. Large ships take longer to change course than do speedboats, but they also can carry more cargo and sail through the big storms.

APPO: Bootstrapping Membership on a Shoestring

Managers tell me all the time that their operation is too small to build a membership organization. I tell them to look at APPO and Cathi Nelson.

For Cathi Nelson, 2007 was the year of the incredible shrinking paycheck. After 17 years of steady income as a successful creative memories consultant, by 2007 she could no longer make a living. Digital photography had killed the scrapbooking industry (and Creative Memories itself no longer exists).[1]

Nelson knew that people were going to need to figure out new ways to manage their photos in the digital age, and she began helping them. "I was like a geek squad for digital images," she told me. "I helped people find the images on their computers, scan old pictures, and learn to use the new sites for managing their photos.... And then they started asking for help creating the books, slide shows, and other photo products too. It was a lightbulb moment for me—I realized people needed a photo organizer."[2]

It wasn't long before word got out, and Nelson started getting inquiries not just from customers, but from people who wanted to do what Nelson was doing. In 2009, she set up an online community called the Association of Personal Photo Organizers. For a minimal fee of a few hundred dollars a year, members of APPO gained access to Nelson's best practices, standard presentations to use in marketing their services, and eventually a certification program. With forums to help one another and an ongoing webinar series that helped members build business and develop organizing skills, by 2014 the fledgling association had attracted over 500 professionals from six continents.

Nelson paid her web designer on a monthly plan and eventually invested in simple SaaS software tools to support the site, including YourMembership.com and GoToMeeting.com for her webinars. Otherwise, her expenses have been minimal. APPO has run mostly on Nelson's sweat.

Major manufacturers and service providers in the digital photography world regularly reach out to APPO.

Today, Nelson spends her time helping her members to be successful in their own businesses and marketing the fledgling professional photo organizer industry. With one part-time employee, Nelson has bootstrapped her business. Major manufacturers and service providers in the digital photography world regularly reach out to her to offer discounts and partnerships for her members.

She has organized an annual conference and established a "Save Your Photos Day," teaming up with companies to teach people how to protect their images and videos in case of a disaster. This initiative is both a community education day and a way to educate the world on the importance of personal photo organizers.

What is Nelson's secret to building this successful business without outside money even as she continued to work as a personal photo organizer herself? She spent the most time "at the bottom of the funnel" as we discuss Chapter 5. Before launching the association, she spent a lot of time making sure that people saw value in the membership and on retention. Once she had a great offering, the acquisition was easy—people came through word-of-mouth.

Most importantly, Nelson has always focused on the fact that if she is not providing true value, even if potential customers become members, they are not going to remain members. Because they are all small business owners, the cost of membership is a direct cost to them, so they are always thinking about the cost. Nelson's strength has been her commitment to serving the members and her constant communication to ensure that her members continue to thrive even as the markets change.

The Sierra Club: Rethinking the Benefits of Membership

In contrast to feisty little APPO, the Sierra Club is a blue-chip leader, with over a century of history. The organization has been really successful in making progress toward its mission, which can be summarized as follows:

- To explore, enjoy, and protect the wild places of the earth
- To practice and promote the responsible use of the earth's ecosystems and resources
- To educate and enlist humanity to protect and restore the quality of the natural and human environment
- To use all lawful means to carry out these objectives[3]

Always looking for ways to grow and stay relevant, the Sierra Club has recently invested in taking a fresh look at its membership model, strengthening ongoing ties with its biggest supporters while simultaneously engaging new members.

Michelle Epstein, deputy chief advancement officer at the Sierra Club, is one of the rare people who has seen membership from both the for-profit and the nonprofit sides. Early in her career she worked for Bookspan, the joint venture between Time Warner and Bertelsmann that operated many of the major book clubs in the United States—including Book of the Month Club, Doubleday Book Club, and Literary Guild. Bookspan was the sister company to the BMG CD Club and the Columbia House DVD Club and used a similar model, featuring a parade of catalogs and a negative opt-in process that resulted in packages (with invoices attached) arriving on the doorstep every month.

> *"Too many Membership Economy organizations under-deliver on the promise of membership."*
>
> Michelle Epstein

At Bookspan, Epstein was fascinated by the potential of the membership model and was constantly trying to test ways to make these "clubs" more interpersonal and clublike, instead of just being a source of ongoing book delivery.

"Too many Membership Economy organizations under-deliver on the promise of membership. They need to over-deliver," says Epstein[4] And wherever she goes, she brings this mantra of membership with her, looking for ways to layer value into memberships to offer members connection, benefits, and aspirational identity going beyond a single benefit model.

The Sierra Club, founded in 1892 and with 2.4 million current members and supporters, is one of the largest and most respected environmental advocacy groups in the world. Epstein noticed, however, that many members were so disconnected that they often didn't know their membership had lapsed. Beyond mailings and emails, the truly personal interaction with the organization for many members was simply too sporadic and infrequent.

Given the origins of the organization, it was unfortunate that the connection had become so loose for many members. The Sierra Club's membership recruitment model used to be highly personal, requiring that new members be nominated by another member. Through the 1950s, you had to know someone to join, and the club really felt like a club. Over time, it adopted more direct membership marketing techniques, acquiring more members via mail, phone, and online channels. As it expanded its reach to millions, it had become more of a database of donors and committed environmental supporters than a tightly engaged community. Even though there were (and are) activists in all 50 states, it didn't feel like a club for most members.

Epstein talked to me about a few major initiatives that are transforming the club[5]:

- Rethink benefits of membership to attract more members.
- Build a larger segment of monthly donors. About 5 percent of the Sierra Club members make an automatic monthly donation. (At Greenpeace, the rate is about 50 percent.)
- Incorporate access to a new, free, online activism platform as a draw for people to join the club.

Epstein wants to layer the ongoing membership with profound benefits that encourage members to live more environmentally friendly lifestyles via the products and services that they choose to use. If you ask average members of the Sierra Club why they joined, they will probably talk about wanting to support a specific advocacy effort. Maybe a few will mention the trips the Sierra Club organizes, or *Sierra*, the monthly magazine, but mostly people join for a cause—writing a check as the primary activity.

> In other words, functional benefits are most effective at attracting members; and advocacy comes later.

In the recent article "The Secret of Scale" in the *Stanford Social Innovation Review*, Peter Murray looked at how advocacy organizations achieved true scale and predictable revenue.[6] He found that organizations like AARP and the National Rifle Association (NRA) have expanded to provide lifestyle benefits, like group insurance, product discounts, and access to special events—going well beyond traditional advocacy. He notes that those organizations that provide functional benefits have scaled more effectively and are much larger than organizations that rely primarily on issue advocacy to build their organizations. Once members are attracted to the functional benefits, the organizations are better able to deftly use their databases to engage those members in issue advocacy initiatives. In other words, functional benefits are most effective at attracting members; and advocacy comes later.

This idea echoes Tien Tzuo's idea about building benefits around relationships. The CEO of Zuora has pointed out that even for a traditional brand, marketing is no longer simply about pitching a product; it's about delivering more broadly on the brand promise and doing it in an ongoing, consistent way as products and services continue to evolve. Before individuals become advocates, they need to be engaged with the brand first.

The Sierra Club is applying these ideas and is aggressively looking into benefits and discounts through partnerships that appeal to environmentally aware members. In addition, it has increased its focus on improving the member onboarding experience, welcoming new members, making them aware of benefits, and connecting them to subgroups devoted to specific causes.

To create community and to expand its reach, the Sierra Club has also built an online community. In June 2014, it released a beta version of an online platform called ADDUP.org. This community site integrates Facebook-like social networking features with "click-tivism"—the ability to discover and support a wide range of activist campaigns. The platform also offers opportunities to engage in local events in the physical world. One of the primary goals of the site is to get members (and nonmembers) to engage locally. Initially, the outreach is limited to the Sierra Club's existing members and supporters, but there are all kinds of hooks in the site designed to go viral and bring in friends of members. After the beta phase, it will be open to everyone. In addition, ADDUP participants that are not yet Sierra Club members will receive ongoing emails and messages to encourage joining the parent club.

Leaving Well Enough Alone Is Not Good Enough

Professional societies, trade associations, and other nonprofits are increasingly tinkering with membership offerings. They know that lack of feedback from members does not necessarily indicate satisfaction. Increased fees, decreased perceived benefits, and any technology glitches related to autopay can threaten membership numbers.

Members may not be clamoring for innovation, but they recognize it when they're presented with a pricing change or a value-packed option. Suddenly, a competitor's offering can look shabby by comparison. I'm not naming names, but one of the clunkiest, cobwebbed, old-school (and not in a good way) sites, dead and drab as a bulletin board, belongs to an organization that prides itself on being a computing research innovator. Innovation is not one of the adjectives potential new members are going to think of when they visit that site. And by the way, this organization publishes a magazine 10 times a year—to reach an industry that is changing by the hour.

So how can a professional society, trade association, or nonprofit take advantage of its head start in membership and strengthen relationships so that it can continue to grow?

What We Can Learn from Nonprofits, Professional Societies, and Trade Associations

Nonprofit organizations, associations, advocacy groups, and museums, like all organizations, need to think about constant innovation while staying true to their mission and relevant to their members. Many of the most creative nonprofits are following the lead of the subscription economy in the private sector and are encouraging members to make an automated monthly donation. The benefits to the organization are obvious—predictable revenue, organic retention, and fewer "big transactions" to win.

But there are also ways that the best for-profit Membership Economy companies are learning from nonprofits. Mission-driven, built around members, and committed for the long term, nonprofits demonstrate the stamina, resolve, and focus required for success in the Membership Economy. And while money helps, innovation is mostly a function of understanding and imagination.

Remember

Online communities can complement offline relationships—consider forums, best practices, webinars, and more.

- Look for partnerships with offerings that can supplement your own.
- Even if members say they love your offerings, continue to evaluate and reevaluate your offerings, your membership, your competition, your assets, and your public face.
- You need to understand your ideal member and be worthy of him or her. Continue to grow and evolve in ways that both retain your long-time members and attract new ones. Your future ideal member may not look like or think like yesterday's members. (A hint that your offering is tired: a decline in member acquisitions. That's a red flag even if member retention remains high.)
- Always be on the lookout for new segments to serve. Optimize your offering for every new tier, but limit the number of segments because each one adds cost and effort.
- Be aware of competition, just like other corporate entities. Do you know who your competition is? Think beyond other associations, other nonprofits. Who else delivers attractive services to your members? Who else has their mind-share? Your biggest competitor could be an online publication app, a user group, a software-as-a-service (SaaS), or a virtual community.
- Stay fresh. Make sure your members are not embarrassed to be seen with you or embarrassed to be using your services.

SECTION IV THE MEMBERSHIP ECONOMY AND TRANSFORMATION

In Section III, Membership Economy Organizations Come in All Shapes and Sizes, we see some examples of organizations that have implemented the strategies of the Membership Economy successfully. It's helpful to see best practices and what organizations look like when they are doing well.

However, I think the principles in this book are most helpful at moments *when things are not fine*. Organizations most often invest in joining the Membership Economy when they are at a crossroads. I call them points of inflection—moments when a company's financial situation can either get much better or much worse—when change is imminent. Sometimes these moments are thrust upon organizations via competitive disruption. Other times, organizations make a proactive decision to change their approach when they see a major opportunity or challenge ahead.

There are many drivers that push organizations to transform, but there are a few that you see over and over in the Membership Economy. Section IV focuses on these moments of transformation, outlined in Table IV. My goal is that you will learn how other organizations have gracefully navigated these changes. Also, I want to inspire you to think about how you can use these points of inflection to scale new mountains, as opposed to just filling in holes.

	Why this transition is tricky	What can we learn from this model?
Idea to Start-Up	• "Chicken and egg" problem at launch • High start-up costs of creating the "shared assets" of membership • Establishing value-based pricing for ongoing membership with one-time "extras" • Temptation to be all things to all people	• Start at the bottom of the funnel—be sure there's benefit/product/member alignment before investing in acquisition. • Set a membership-oriented culture from the beginning—titles, language, processes all matter. • If you can't "import a group" to seed your community, you must provide value that is independent of the social benefits. • Don't boil the ocean. Start small and focused with a specific audience. Multiple targets multiply budgets!

Table IV The Membership Economy and Transformation: Key Inflection Points

	Why this transition is tricky	What can we learn from this model?
Start-Up to Mature Company	• What got you here won't get you there (team, processes)	• Being known as "edgy" or "cool" is a double-edged sword—speeds early growth, but can't work as a lasting brand.
	• Mistakes that seemed small at the outset are magnified as the organization scales • Challenge of moving from the single big idea to continuous innovation • New skills needed, and maybe new culture	• As you grow, you need to evolve your funnel into an hourglass, expanding the engagement and impact of members. • Once you've proven the model, and acquisition and retention are working, aggressively seek to automate processes and build structure—the start-up pace and "bespoke approach" to customer satisfaction is not sustainable.
Offline to Online	• Challenge to drive offline benefits through online channel • New skills needed, and maybe new culture • Emotionally difficult to jettison legacy systems	• Members expect to be able to access their communities online. Period. Nearly every offline benefit has an online corollary, and usually at a lower cost than the real-world version. If you're not providing it, someone else will. • Online technology extends the connection among members and between members and organizations. • Online technology enables greater engagement and stickiness by building behaviors into members' daily routines.
Ownership to Access	• Likely to lose some members who don't fit squarely into the new target member model • Short-term revenue decline from big and lumpy transactions to small, recurring payments • New skills needed and maybe new culture	• Be transparent about change, communicate clearly to stakeholders. • Consider grandfathering ownership model, at least for corner-case customers. • Research and analyze impact across all segments. • Expect pushback if you're forcing customers to new model.

(continued)

Table IV The Membership Economy and Transformation: Key Inflection Points

	Why this transition is tricky	What can we learn from this model?
Steady State to Competitive Disruption	• Successful company often (nearly always) feels blindsided by competition • No time to prepare—in reactive rather than proactive mode • Temptation to fill holes rather than build mountains • New skills needed, and maybe new culture	• As former Intel CEO Andy Grove says, "Only the paranoid survive"—ask the question Dawn Sweeney, CEO of the National Restaurant Association, asks her team every few months: "If you wanted to put us out of business, what would you do?" • Stay close to members and listen carefully. Try to say yes when you hear the same request repeatedly. • When you find yourself in a competitive state, do what News International CMO Katie Vanneck Smith did—use it as an opportunity to rethink your whole model and leapfrog your competition. • Consider buying innovative start-ups as a means to absorb fresh models—be willing to cannibalize your own business.

(continued)

Table IV The Membership Economy and Transformation: Key Inflection Points

17 | From Idea to Start-Up

Start-ups can have a very tough time with the Membership Economy because of the "chicken and egg" problem. They need a critical mass of members before they can provide value to the first member. Yet, many membership organizations have successfully navigated this challenge.

What too few entrepreneurs realize is how important it is to figure out all the details around pricing, value proposition, and customer acquisition and retention before they invest in growth. A compelling start-up offers something valuable on the first day. *Or* it needs to bring in a whole group of members at once. (Or both.)

To gain insights about how to go from idea to start-up, we look at some companies that are big and successful now like LinkedIn, Relay-Rides, and Facebook, to see how they established themselves in the early days.

If you are thinking about starting a Membership Economy business, whether online or offline, this chapter can show you tactics for the early days that can get you up and running. You will see that many organizations have been able to prove that their concepts work, even with a small budget. Keeping things simple—especially with membership—is the right way to start. Focus on the key market and harness viral growth. Finally, it's critical to do a lot of testing while you're small, because the bigger you get, the harder it is to turn the ship in another direction.

LinkedIn: Start with Clear Brand Identity and a Forever Transaction Idea

We discuss LinkedIn's use of freemium and leveraging a core engine of free memberships to build a huge revenue-generating business in Chapter 12. Now, let's go into some detail about how it started.

Allen Blue is one of the founders and vice president of product management. He is responsible for LinkedIn's content, community, and communication. Blue told me the company started with a value proposition not that different from that of many professional associations. "We knew we wanted to capture relationships between people, and not just the person's content itself. We wanted to make sure that there's an ongoing value from that first point on."[1]

As LinkedIn designed the organization, founders thought about where they wanted to be in the long term, as well as what they needed to do to get things started.

The LinkedIn founding team was thoughtful from the start about the kind of organization they wanted to build, improving on the models they had built in the past. Blue, with cofounders Reid Hoffman and Jean-Luc Vaillant, had ideas about the kind of culture that was needed.

Language mattered from the beginning. Blue remembers, "Just before we launched in April 2003, we began having a conversation internally about how we needed to talk to our members. How to address them. Members? Users? We knew subscription would eventually be part of our business model. Most importantly, we wanted to provide an experience for each individual user—so basically that they would recognize value to themselves and act on it by inviting other members. We needed to establish a long-term value proposition."

Another important element was building a "forever transaction" and a true relationship with each member. Blue and Hoffman both had had experience working at dating sites—but there, once members found their soul mates, they were out. The system had no further value. With people's careers, however, "We knew we could have you for 40 years—if we made it clear we could provide value."

Blue commented on the power of the brand, which he defines as the expectation set by the enterprise during early interactions; it informs expectations regarding the entire relationship. He cautions organizations to think about the brand early on. It can be hard to change people's expectations once those expectations have been set.

> *To become a member, there must be some kind of vetting and initiation which results in a change in status.*

Blue thinks of membership as a relationship between a person and an organization of other people, where basically there's a barrier between members and nonmembers. To become a member, there must be some kind of vetting and initiation which results in a change in status. The member goes from being someone with little access, value, and power to someone with those things, through his or her participation or investment or both.

Founders of LinkedIn chose the word "membership" over "user" to describe the relationships they wanted to establish with the beneficiaries of LinkedIn. While Blue doesn't see the language of membership as the most important element in LinkedIn's success, he does believe words have an impact on how employees think about the people using their offerings. The word "membership" transforms a purely transactional feeling into a lasting relationship with an entity. Blue believes that language has power in organizing efforts of people and connotations in the business design. When you start with "user," he says, what you create is more tool-like, more high tech. When you start with "member," it's a bit more high touch, a bit more focused on a member's needs and values.

LinkedIn's challenge in getting started had to do with providing value on the first day, which it did by letting people use the site as a place to store and share their résumés. Over time, it layered on the value of the community—making LinkedIn a place where people could manage professional connections. Today, LinkedIn is much more—it's almost a requirement for any professional and provides a broad range of services and benefits for professionals, but also for sales people, recruiters, and market researchers. It's important to remember the early days and how the company started with a narrow value proposition and the right infrastructure, culture, and vision for growth.

Like LinkedIn, RelayRides had a challenge moving from the idea stage to implementation. While LinkedIn simply needed to provide one point of value in a professional's life in exchange for a résumé, RelayRides had to convince people to let strangers drive their car. How they did it, through a localized approach and high touch, is instructive.

RelayRides: Recruit Members One by One

In 1999, Alex Benn, a young Stanford-educated lawyer, left Cooley Godward, one of the leading law firms in Silicon Valley, after having met Pierre Omidyar at eBay. eBay, the person-to-person auction site for collectibles, had recently gone public. Omidyar needed a great, business-minded attorney to help the company grow faster through partnerships and acquisitions so that he could quickly take peer trading to the masses.

> Omidyar explained to Benn his view that "people are basically good."

Benn was initially reluctant to adopt Omidyar's perspective. A street-smart New Jersey native, Benn describes growing up with a worldview that "everyone's out to get you." It was hard for him to believe that a large group of strangers would behave fairly and honestly, especially behind the shield of the Internet where anonymity is common. But Omidyar explained to Benn his view that "people are basically good." Benn joined the young membership organization, where he executed many of its formative partnerships and over 15 merger-and-acquisition transactions, representing more than $1 billion in value. His experiences at eBay sold him on Omidyar's optimistic view of humanity.

Benn shared his long-ranging perspective on membership and community with me: "People—generally—go out of their way for strangers. . . . There may be cultural differences, but as a planet and a species, we are alike in that way. . . . If we couldn't band together as tribes, we never would have gotten here."[2]

Today, Benn is the COO of RelayRides, often called the "Airbnb" of car-sharing. RelayRides is the nation's largest car-sharing marketplace, enabling owners to rent their cars out to people who need them. Relay-Rides is based on the idea that there is unused value stored in cars, an expensive, underutilized asset, and that advances in technology could unlock that value.

Figuring out the technical side of RelayRides, using geotracking, big data, and General Motors' Onstar's remote car unlocking system to track and unlock members' cars was the easier part. The harder part was convincing owners to rent out their cars and convincing people who needed a car to feel safe driving a car that belonged to a stranger. It was expecting a lot to ask members to let the organization put technology into their cars and make their precious personal asset available for rental at any time. RelayRides initially had to recruit each member in a very hands-on, personal way, calling each individually and discussing the process before the community began growing virally. Eventually, the company moved to an automated system, once it had critical mass and a proven concept, but early on, it actually brought in drivers and owners one by one, and city by city.

RelayRides had a tough time getting started because it needed to establish trust. Later it could rely more on word-of-mouth and the brand it had built.

Benn is often asked, "Is there a future in sharing?" ("Sharing" being the buzzword used to describe companies like RelayRides and Airbnb that act as marketplaces for the rental of personal property.) His response is to look at the past as a way to anticipate the future.

He takes a long view, starting with early civilization and pointing out how each innovation in shared infrastructure strengthened and expanded the way we build trusting communities. Shared roads, communications advances, currency, and legal protections have constantly increased the span of trust. Today we can build highly trusting relationships with organizations and individuals we've never met.

RelayRides started with the trust between real people and over time was able to expand that approach to a digital community. By staying focused and being willing to tinker with the model and use a labor-intensive approach until it reached critical mass, RelayRides was able to build a totally new model.

Facebook did something similar, growing cluster by cluster, but in that case, it started with a community that already existed in the physical world.

Facebook: Start with a Homogeneous Group

The first members of Facebook were Harvard undergraduates who attended the college when Mark Zuckerberg was a student there. Harvard had long distributed so-called facebooks, bound books with names and pictures of everyone in a dorm or class, indexed by first name, last name, hometown, and major. Students used them to identify new friends and potential hookups although that certainly was not the administration's intent. During Zuckerberg's time at Harvard, the university was experimenting with bringing the facebook's content online, in a very rudimentary way. According to Harvard's student paper, *The Harvard Crimson*, Zuckerberg hacked into several websites of Harvard dorms, known as "Houses," to gather the photos, and then wrote the codes to compute rankings after every vote.[3]

Zuckerberg first created a "hot or not" copycat site (vote for one of two pictures) called "Facemash." From there, he continued to tinker, using student data to build his next site, known in its early days as thefacebook.com, turning it into what is today the basis for the Facebook we know and love. Facebook initially grew school by school, building a membership cluster by cluster. Facebook needed people who knew and trusted each other in order to provide the social network experience. Without other members who knew one another, the site had little value to an individual, so bringing on a group of members was critical.

It's hard to think of a time when Facebook was just an idea and "the Facebook" had little meaning outside Harvard University. If not for Zuckerberg's ability to make his model relevant to the homogenous group of people who were the very first to use his fledgling service, it never would have expanded to provide the breadth and depth of services it has today.

Netflix: Pick One Key Benefit and Deliver It to a Focused Audience

Netflix had a different challenge. While not heavily committed to community interaction, Netflix had an equally ambitious idea—to make sure that its subscribers always had three great DVDs on hand. In the early days, the company had several benefits that it could have marketed. These could have included the convenience of having DVDs delivered to one's home, the range of movies available through the central distribution center, and the ability to keep a queue of DVDs on file so people would get a movie that they actually wanted whenever it was available.

Many companies make the mistake of wanting to talk about all the benefits right from the first day. There are two problems with this approach. First, if you promise too many things, it is hard to deliver on all of them. Second, if you promise too many things, customers get confused and might not be able to find the benefit that really matters to them.

> Too many small organizations are unwilling to invest early on in market research.

Netflix kept things very simple in the early days. It focused on one key benefit: no late fees. This benefit positioned the company against the big video stores, especially Blockbuster, and appealed to consumers who were already renting lots of movies. It was also a benefit that Netflix could deliver on in the early days. Later, Netflix touted other benefits, like 2-day delivery, 10,000-plus titles, and original content. But in the early days, the focus was on late fees to win over disgruntled Blockbuster customers.

Netflix also used a simple pricing model—with one primary option for all members. Keeping the subscription simple reduced barriers to entry and friction in the sign-up flow. Netflix invested heavily in member research from the outset and was able to adjust offers and messaging in response to the research. Too many small organizations are unwilling to invest early on in market research and therefore either trip into failure or stumble into success. Early in an organization's lifecycle, talking to prospects and customers is among the most important investments. By staying focused, solving one problem really well, and communicating that benefit, Netflix was able to get from idea, to start-up, to mature industry leader.

What Can We Learn from This Model?

Start-ups are sometimes stymied because they can't offer the full benefits envisioned by the founders from day one. And yet there are many ways to start with a focused or even mass-customized strategy as a first step toward achieving the full vision.

Every organization needs to provide value to the first member. Sometimes that's like LinkedIn, starting with a single offer and expanding over time. Sometimes it is by limiting growth or growing region by region to ensure that new members will feel the benefits of the community, like RelayRides. Other times, an organization uses a manual approach until it has confidence that it can automate the process and build out the model. In the Membership Economy, splashy is not necessary—steady growth is.

Remember

- Start at the bottom of the acquisition funnel. Be sure benefits, products, and members align before you invest in acquiring members.
- Establish a membership-oriented culture within the organization from the beginning—titles, language, and processes all matter.
- If you can't "import a group" to seed your community, you must provide value independent of the benefits that a growing membership can offer prospective members.
- Start small and focused with a specific audience. Multiple targets multiply budgets!
- When you're getting started, it's okay to use a manual, labor-intensive approach until you figure out what process is going to work for you.

18 From Start-Up to Mature Organization

Fast-growing start-up organizations often have the wind at their backs and are looking ahead to a clear horizon. It's precisely at that time that they can best bear major innovation and risk. Sometimes changes can rock the boat, but in the long term, prudent risk can position a good company to become great. Try a few small experiments with big potential, and see what happens.

Successful start-ups home in on their growth strategy early, often relying on instincts and their cool factor to attract early adopters who, in turn, refer their friends. Between organic, viral growth of some organizations and word-of-mouth of others, hot companies can go quickly from start-up to giant. And because they don't look like a threat, small companies can often fly under the radar for a while before their competitors notice and react.

The challenge start-ups face is what to do when they reach critical mass. At that point, they can't rely on their stealth or their cool factor any more. The trend spotters have moved on, as they do with fashion or nightclubs. Now the organization has to stand up to the scrutiny of the larger mainstream market. While the growth rate might slow, organizations need to make sure they don't fall into decline. They need to seamlessly transition themselves into a mature, "grown up" organization. Some organizations lose their way in this transition while others successfully continue to reinvent themselves.

Growing from an adolescent membership organization into a mature one is painful. You need more structure in the organization. You need a brand promise that's bigger than "the next new thing." You need to figure out how to stay relevant to the members. And you need to learn how to build innovation into the organization instead of relying on the founder's initial great idea and intuition.

If your organization is a rocket ship and people come to you because you're cool, under the radar, or a disruptive star, make sure you have a plan for what you're going to do when you're no longer the new thing. Because that day will come. In this chapter, we look at Pandora and Salesforce .com, two companies now firmly in the mainstream that gracefully managed growth from disruptor to industry leader.

Pandora: Becoming Part of the Conversation

The seeds for Pandora were sown in the Music Genome Project, which began in 2000 and continues today as "the most comprehensive analysis of music ever undertaken." A team of music analysts have been listening to and analyzing songs (now numbering over a million) across up to 450 distinct characteristics including every detail of melody, harmony, instrumentation, rhythm, vocals, lyrics, and more.

Pandora uses this database to select songs based on a person's preferences to create a personalized radio experience. A listener can type the name of a song or artist into Pandora and the Music Genome Project uses its database to find songs with interesting musical similarities, creating, in real time, a "station"[1] unique to that listener's taste.

After five years of painstaking development, Pandora launched its consumer-facing service in the fall of 2005. Founder Tim Westergren viewed it as a big company from the beginning. Although the company briefly tried a pure paid model, it quickly realized that with radio's well-established history of being free, consumers demanded an ad-supported offering. It was this free version that supercharged growth and rapidly turned Pandora into a household name. At the time of its IPO filing in 2011, an event that often signals the transition of a company from cool start-up to mature player, Pandora reported 80 million registered listeners.[2] Since then, listener growth has continued. In 2014, the company reported breaking 250 million registered members.[3]

> *"Edgy is another way of saying a lot of people aren't going to fit here. We want to make room for everyone."*
> Tim Westergren

Part of this growth is the result of Pandora's focus on being a mainstream product from the earliest days. Westergren told me, "We have never sought to be edgy. Edgy brands are usually weak brands. Edgy is another way of saying a lot of people aren't going to fit here. We want to make room for everyone. Edgy is way overrated." In other words, if you don't try to be cool to start, you don't risk becoming uncool.

Westergren says that respect for the individual is in the organization's core DNA. Pandora's principles are codified with the intent of informing decision making and conduct across the organization. Employees learn the principles formally at "Pandora University," a two-day introduction led by executive staff and senior leaders that exposes new hires to all aspects of Pandora's business. All employees are expected to respect all members, communicate regularly, and strive to make them feel welcome, regardless of age, hipness, or musical preferences. Once employees join Pandora, they become part of the day-to-day conversation with listeners. "If you're carrying your Pandora bag on the subway," says Westergren, "people will ask you about it. For an employee, it's incredibly gratifying."[4]

> *@pandora_radio just got six songs in a row that I love #amazing #powerofmusic*

Pandora works overtime to treat every listener—paid or free—like a member. It views communication as an opportunity, not a cost, and is committed to answering every single email with a personal reply. Westergren says, "Our most active listeners communicate to us, write us poetry, bake cakes, send us photographs. They do things to express their love for the product. Spontaneous and unsolicited demonstrations of affection are powerful for employees. Self-selected ambassadors become walking evangelists." Typical tweets paint a picture of loyal listeners who feel like "forever transaction" members:

"I love it when @pandora_radio knows just what I need to hear. It's like a hug from a friend."

> I have enjoyed your 'product' for a few years now. I broke my neck in a cycling accident in December 2013, and listening to your Smooth Jazz station helped me through some trying times in my recovery. Your continuous stream of calming music was just the non-addictive medication I needed. Thanks for being there for me!

"My father was very sick, and died when I was 16. The one thing I remembered most was his love of country music and him listening to his record player. Your station brought me to a place I have never been before. It was as if he was there beside me, I was actually looking for him, with so many things to say, and waiting for Mother to call us to supper. From the bottom of my Heart, Thank you for those moments."

"Someone I spoke to at a call center had talked about how much she loved Pandora," explained Westergren. "Everyone in her office had different music tastes, but they all used it. I sent her Pandora T-shirts. She loved them and handed them out and now is the Pandora Lady at work. People will write blog posts and tell stories of personal experiences—the way Pandora soothed loved ones when someone passed away, or while overseas to stay in touch with family, or while giving birth."

At Pandora, the acquisition funnel is more of an hourglass, as members recruit their friends and feel like they're truly an extension of the company. Beyond these online connections, Westergren hosts town hall meetings. These open, unscripted gatherings, which Westergren began hosting shortly after the launch, give listener-members the chance to interact directly and personally with the company. They started small, with just a few dozen attendees, but now, over 500 town halls later, hundreds attend, and they can last for hours. "Our town hall meetings have everyone—13-year-olds, 85-year-olds, punk rockers, and Rastafarians. Everyone is sitting together, and it feels like a unified group. Music is the common experience."

Westergren points out that "a personalized service has to lay out the welcome mat for everyone. We made it a welcoming place for everyone, no matter your taste and your tech savvy." Some of that in-person communication has catalyzed growth—much of it word-of-mouth between friends. Advocates also use more formal channels, including blog posts, chat rooms, and forums. Westergren has experienced this for himself when interacting with individual listeners, hearing things like, "Thanks so much—I told all my friends," or, "Thanks for the T-shirt—I wore it to my friend's birthday party this weekend and got so many comments." In this day and age, one individual can influence many people.

He says that his experience didn't feel like a transition from start-up to big company. Because Westergren always knew what kind of organization he wanted to create and stayed true to that vision, he was ready when Pandora reached the mainstream. By offering a clear value and a consistent brand promise, Pandora has been able to transition from start-up to mature organization—as has Salesforce.com.

Salesforce.com: Consumerizing the Enterprise

In 1999, former Oracle salesman Marc Benioff started a groundbreaking company to help salespeople manage their relationships. His company, Salesforce.com, was built on a model radically different from other business software companies. In fact, the first marketing campaign featured the word "software" with a line drawn through it, implying that its "software" wasn't actually being packaged as software at all.

> The software-as-a-service model meant that the software didn't have to be downloaded, managed, or upgraded.

Benioff's insight was that advances in Internet technology had made it easy for nontechnical people (even salespeople!) to purchase business software, a revolutionary idea. Sales reps could subscribe to access software without needing help from their IT department. The software would update itself, and the sales reps could use the software without their parent company's involvement. This was the promise of the cloud—easy, efficient, and secure. This idea alone helped Salesforce.com grow at lightning speed.[5]

When Salesforce.com came along, it was one of the first software-as-a-service models. This meant that the vendor managed the software implementation and that the customer didn't have to worry about the responsibilities of ownership—a big advance from prior business models.

Also Salesforce.com used a new strategy to seed the market, now known as "consumerization of the enterprise." Instead of selling to the larger enterprises, Salesforce.com targeted the salespeople themselves. The salespeople acted like consumers, making a decision on their own behalf, subscribing to Salesforce.com to make their own lives easier.

Salespeople could actually buy it as individuals, for a relatively low price that they could expense. The Salesforce.com solution was first designed to help the salespeople, not with a primary focus on the corporation. As a result, the salespeople loved it. It was easy to buy and powerful to use.

Even though Salesforce.com initially targeted salespeople, the end users of their solution, from the beginning, the start-up envisioned partnerships with vendors who would sell related apps and IT firms that would implement the Salesforce.com solution enterprise-wide. "Salesforce.com wanted to foster collaboration between Salesforce.com and individual partners and customers but also among the partners and customers," says Leyla Seka, senior vice president and general manager of Desk.com at Salesforce.com.[6] What was smart about Salesforce.com's strategy was that it, like Pandora, had the long-term strategy in mind, even as it was in the start-up phase. Rather than "managing the brand" in the traditional sense, it encouraged everyone in the user/developer community to communicate with each other.

Salesforce.com began to transition into its next phase, enterprise sales, once it had seeded the market with users and achieved critical mass. The company began to aggregate data on which companies had the most salespeople using Salesforce.com and then sent a representative to talk with the corporate employer. The pitch was, "Look how many of your salespeople are already buying Salesforce.com—wouldn't you like to gain the control and price break that come from central purchasing?"

From there, it continued to engage its community, building forums to generate conversation online and listening carefully to the good and the bad news. "We've done interesting things at Salesforce.com," said Seka. "With every product release, we incorporate features that our community members have voted on through our 'True to the Core' program."

Today, Salesforce.com is the corporate standard for customer relationship management, purchased at the enterprise level. The company's unique strategy of finding prospects by providing direct value to the individual users of their "nonsoftware"—the salespeople—was key in helping it grow from a scrappy start-up into a mature company. From there, extending its marketing efforts to reach the enterprises where these individuals worked was an easy next step. Salesforce.com has since grown to look more like a traditional enterprise SaaS company, with a big sales organization and big annual subscription contracts. But it has kept its membership orientation.

In addition to providing the initial suite of services and community for salespeople, the company also has invested heavily in a community for developers. Its AppExchange is a marketplace where Salesforce.com customers can download free or paid applications that increase the value of the data customers keep in the Salesforce.com system. These apps are vetted by the Salesforce.com organization, and the app developers and users further strengthen the community around Salesforce.com.

What's great about the AppExchange and Salesforce.com's developer community, DeveloperForce.com, is that the partners get immediate feedback on their apps and can rapidly improve their offerings in response to what they hear. The community mitigates risk that customers won't like new apps because the app developers know they will be told how to make them better. Often, partners even join forces and develop new offerings in response to community discussions.

For many sales and marketing professionals, as well as for the application developers who build solutions that complement Salesforce.com, the Salesforce.com community is core to its success, conferring status, publicizing job opportunities, and building important peer relationships.

Access has trumped ownership, turning the software business model upside down and revolutionizing an entire industry. Salesforce.com continues to reinvent itself—it's no longer just about delivering for sales users. In 2014 Forbes named Salesforce.com the world's most innovative company, for a record fourth consecutive year.[7] It's Salesforce.com's commitment to innovation that has allowed it to continue evolving and expanding, going from innovative start-up to mature industry leader.

What Can We Learn from This Model?

If your organization feels like a rocket ship and members flock to join you because they describe your organization with words like "cool," "under the radar," or "disruptive star"—make sure you have a plan. Know what you're going to do when you're no longer what Membership Economy pioneer Jim Clark (founder of many companies including Netscape, WebMD, and myCFO) once called "the new new thing." Because that day is coming.

> This transition from start-up to mature organization is deceptively difficult.

This transition from start-up to mature organization is deceptively difficult. Everyone knows that getting started is hard, but most people don't realize how many companies nose-dive after a fantastic launch phase. Organizations need to expect and prepare for potential hazards, including slowing revenue growth, conflicts between new and existing members, and increasing competition from both the big players who are finally noticing you and new up-starts who see *you* as the dinosaur.

Moving from the single big idea to continuous innovation is tricky, but critical. The information here is relevant even for organizations that have successfully managed the transition to relative maturity. The same techniques that help transition a start-up to a success can be applied to incorporating a skunkworks endeavor into the larger organization. After all, we've seen casualties of the Membership Economy, firms that had survived the transition from start-up to mature organization only to stumble or crash (Yahoo!, MySpace, Ask Jeeves, LoudCloud).

The best Membership Economy organizations have learned to evolve. Generally, they have solid infrastructure, predictable revenues, metrics that they can count on, and experienced leadership. The challenge they face is precisely this: their own success. Many of the casualties of the Membership Economy had already made it past the challenges of starting up and growing into a successful business.

Remember

- Being known as "edgy" or "cool" is a double-edged sword—it speeds early growth but can't work as a lasting brand.
- As you grow, you need to evolve your funnel into an hourglass (see Chapter 5), expanding the engagement and impact of members.
- Once you've proven the model and acquisition and retention are working, aggressively seek to automate processes and build structure.
- Evaluate what major change you can make to stay edgy to at least some people.
- Consider what new benefits you can capitalize on because you've become mainstream.
- Build some protection against the biggest players who haven't seemed to have noticed you—they're about to put you in their sights.

19

From Offline to Online

Virtually every membership organization has some level of online activity. However, many are missing huge opportunities to engage fully online. Through technology, organizations can extend benefits beyond the limitations of face-to-face contact. It is possible to create new opportunities while lowering costs for members. Moving from offline to online actually requires a change in attitude though. Some organizations with an online presence haven't fully moved to an online mindset. It's not something you do once. It's a different way to think about engaging with members.

The companies discussed in this chapter—Weight Watchers, News Corp, and the Field Museum—were already online before they launched their online initiatives. However, these companies hadn't yet fully incorporated the online experience into their business model.

The transition of extending an existing membership from just offline to online is tricky. Often, offline benefits don't translate well online. Also, members might not want to move online. Ideally, organizations make the transition gradually and provide lots of choices along the way. The online experience may look totally different from the way the offline one did, and in fact may attract new target segments. As with any major transition, planning for constant tinkering, especially in the early days, is critical. The one thing most companies that have moved from offline to online agree on is that things didn't go as smoothly as expected. So budgeting time and money for unexpected challenges is important. Despite the challenges of making this transition, it is one that nearly every offline Membership Economy organization has had to grapple with or is working through now. Any organization that does not provide a meaningful online experience (not just an online presence) is at a major disadvantage. Figuring out how to harness the myriad technological advances of the past few years can lead to tremendous new opportunities—and not figuring the transition out means almost certain failure.

Enticing or requiring subscribers to change their behaviors can require tough choices. Organizations making these transitions risk losing members when they jettison legacy services and systems too quickly or require too much change at once. Nevertheless, it's possible to make the transition with grace and ultimately to turn the online offer into an engine for growth, as Weight Watchers and News Corp demonstrate.

Weight Watchers: Adding the Cloud to the Storefront

Weight Watchers is one of the best examples of a successful membership organization that has continually evolved to meet its members' needs, including making the transition from a traditional membership business model to an online one. The company is driven by a simple, unchanging mission: to help people reach and maintain a healthy weight. In the 1960s, my grandfather was one of its first (he always said *the* first) male meeting leaders—as part of the company's fledgling efforts to become relevant to men as well as women. Nearly 40 years

One of its most innovative changes has been leveraging technology to dramatically reinvent the way it serves its members.

later, I joined a very different Weight Watchers to get healthy after my daughter was born in 2001. Weight Watchers continues to evolve.

Today, Weight Watchers is clearly the dominant company among weight loss centers and programs, banking north of $1.5 billion each year.[1] It is at least three times larger than its primary competitors, Nutrisystem and Jenny Craig. Weight Watchers has about 8 million website visitors per month and 1.72 million paid online subscribers.[2]

Weight Watchers has always used a membership model, requiring ongoing subscription-like payments and emphasizing community. Members who successfully lose weight are invited to become lifetime (free) members and sometimes are recruited to lead their own weight loss meetings. Weight Watchers has continued to innovate. Through its expansion to an online membership model, it has been able to dramatically reinvent the way it serves its members.

Dave Kirchhoff, the former CEO, told me that he is a lifetime member of Weight Watchers and has been at his goal weight since 2009. He wrote about this side benefit of his 13 years with the company in his book *Weight Loss Boss, How to Finally Win at Losing—and Take Charge in an Out-of-Control Food World* (Rodale Books, 2012). In January 2000, when Weight Watchers recruited Kirchhoff from PepsiCo where he worked in the corporate strategy group helping the Tropicana business, the intellectual challenge of taking one of the world's most successful membership communities online appealed to him. He knew he faced several major challenges:

> "If it actually helps people achieve this difficult-to-achieve goal, why should it be ad supported? You need to have skin in the game."
> Dave Kirchhoff

- *Awareness.* No one knew Weight Watchers had an online presence.
- *Pricing.* Ad-supported or subscription?
- *Offering.* Online/offline hybrid or online only?

The company decided on a subscription model, despite the pressure to offer an experience that was fully ad-supported. Kirchhoff recalls the decision being difficult, since all the other weight loss companies seemed to be signing up to do free ad-supported deals with Yahoo! and the other portals. "My view was if our product actually helps people achieve this difficult-to-achieve goal, why should it be ad supported? Why should some random pharmacy or food company sponsor your weight loss? Besides, you need to have skin in the game."

It decided to offer a choice to members—online, offline, or a hybrid. To its surprise, in the early days, most people coming to the online site preferred the fully online solution or the offline-only solution—the hybrid solution didn't take hold until later years.

With a lot of testing and a little bit of luck, Weight Watchers built a model that took off. Kirchhoff said he knew within two months that it had a winner. It surveyed users constantly, using traditional consumer product metrics, to determine if they felt their product exceeded expectations, was worth the money, and was something they would recommend. For the first few years, the company would spend 90 cents of every dollar earned on product development—effectively betting the whole business on continuous innovation to improve the quality of the online experience.

> Too many product managers rely on instinct and gut instead of actual behavioral data.

The driving product development philosophy was to build tools and features that were based on observed member behaviors. The people on the team watched what members were doing on their own and made it easier for them to do it. They started message boards, looked for microcommunities that formed, and created content and experiences for the most active of these microcommunities. They noticed that members were using other sites like Geocities to blog about their weight loss journeys, so Weight Watchers Online created its own blog function. What was interesting was that the features that were most valued by the online members were totally different from the features in the offline program. Most notably, the online program did not have a "meeting" model, the cornerstone of the traditional Weight Watchers program.

Kirchhoff encouraged product managers to become anthropologists. Too many product managers rely on instinct and gut instead of actual behavioral data—which is silly, especially in online communities when there's so much data available to learn exactly what members care about. By keeping an open mind about how its "weekly meeting" and the rest of its traditional approach could be reimagined, even replaced, to enable online members to have the same great weight loss results, Weight Watchers was able to dramatically extend its reach.

Like Weight Watchers, News Corp had a strong brand and history and saw that it needed to think differently about the online extension of its offline brand.

News Corp: Focusing on What Digital Enables

In June 2014, Katie Vanneck-Smith, the chief marketing officer of News UK, was promoted to chief customer officer and global managing director of Dow Jones. No one was surprised at the promotion of the longtime News Corp employee. Vanneck-Smith had already led *The Times*, *The Sunday Times*, and *The Sun*'s marketing organizations into the digital era and transformed their direct relationship with readers through the development of Times+ and Sun+ membership and paywall offerings.[3]

Prior to Vanneck-Smith's tenure as CMO, marketing had been a lower priority for the organization, as it is with most newspaper companies. The traditional wisdom is that circulation is the number that matters, composed of home delivery and newsstand sales. Circulation drives ad sales and prices, which have historically been their primary revenue source.

> *Once readers started getting their news online, their attitudes and expectations about pricing and value changed dramatically.*

Vanneck-Smith was overseeing News Corp's addition of a digital platform for news. Recognizing that once readers started getting their news online, their attitudes and expectations about pricing and value would change dramatically, she began rethinking the company's offerings.

To create what was needed, she first strove to change the culture, if not of the whole company, at least of her team. She said, "We'll need far more of a start-up mentality—more opportunism, more experimentation, more collaboration across our global businesses and the content we produce."[4]

The company hired young marketers with expertise in social and digital promotion, invited key tech team members to sit in the marketing space, and blended the sales and marketing roles to focus more broadly on customer lifetime value.

Instead of thinking about circulation and advertising, she focused on creating bundles of content and value that were consistent with News Corp's various brands. Some of these bundles were a mix of digital and print editions, while some included untraditional offerings—like a tablet device or a subscription to Spotify, the digital music service, with playlists created by the journalists to complement the reading experience. The whole organization also started to use the language of membership instead of subscription, emphasizing the emotional connection it has with its readers.

In addition, Vanneck-Smith sought unusual ways to connect with members. For example, once a new reader signs up, News UK—a British newspaper publisher and subsidiary of News Corp—sends the new member a customized personal invitation to meet with the editor.[5] And it invited a few hundred *Sun Times* readers to a "cocktails and canapes" event which featured a war photographer—access to a very special experience for members.

The idea was that moving from offline to digital was about more than putting the newspaper online, but rather taking advantage of digital technology to extend the brand's reach and value. Instead of thinking of the transition as a catch-up exercise, Vanneck-Smith thought of digital as an enabler for value and began to focus on the lifetime value of the customer instead of ad sales and circulation revenue.

The result of her efforts has been that readers seem willing to pay for the digital bundles, even after over a decade of free digital. As with

Weight Watchers, News Corp made a conscious decision to charge for the value that it creates, focusing on delivering an ongoing experience worth paying for. While it is too early to measure the financial impact on the company, News Corp's commitment to its digital transformation is a key part of its public vision for the future.

The transition from offline to online is not limited to corporations. Nonprofits need to figure out how to extend their reach and value through technology. One innovative example is the Field Museum—where major innovation came about as a result of a superuser's brainstorm.

The Field Museum: Embracing a Member's Creativity

Many museum directors and curators have mixed feelings about outreach and marketing to members. On the one hand, they know that without engagement from their communities, they have little reason to exist (and often no means to exist). On the other hand, sometimes it feels as if the business objectives are at odds with the organization's mission.

This kind of two-way communication between the organization and its members can lead to innovations, large and small.

The Field Museum of Natural History is a notable exception. Located in Chicago, the Field Museum is one of the largest natural history museums in the world, attracting over 2 million visitors annually. The institution has aggressively invested in technology to augment its century-old strategies for connecting with its audience.

In May 2013, the Field Museum announced a new partnership with Emily Glaslie. She is the creator of the YouTube channel "The Brain Scoop." Emily had been hired as the Field's "chief curiosity correspondent." Now, every week or two, Emily posts a five- to ten-minute video about something cool at the museum. Usually, about 50,000 people watch it. Dozens, if not hundreds, of people post comments, mostly positive. Many follow up with further questions about the video. Talk about building awareness and engagement in your museum's content!

This idea didn't come from the Field Museum itself. A museum member contacted the museum staff members, letting them know about Emily's program and suggesting that the museum do something similar. This kind of two-way communication between the organization and its members can lead to innovations, large and small.

On her blog, Brain Scoop with Emily Graslie,[6] Emily described her new role as, "Better than going to an amusement park and not having to wait in lines. It's better than meeting your favorite author and getting his autograph. It's better than a first kiss. It's better than cake and brownies." The Field Museum is pretty thrilled too—attracting a notoriously under-represented audience of girls ages 13 to 18, lots of media attention, and a new way to engage with fans around the world.

This new initiative did not represent a change in attitude or core relationship with members, but was a great example of constant tinkering and small experiments that have big potential.

What Can We Learn from This Model?

Members expect to be able to access their communities online. Period. If you're not providing this access, someone else will. Asking members to change their behaviors can be tricky, so offering additional opportunities to engage rather than forcing change is the best way to go. And whether small changes, as with the Field Museum, or entire models of engagement, as with Weight Watchers Online, using a transition to online as a catalyst to provide new sources of benefit with an organization they belong to is appreciated.

Remember

- Be willing to change your approach in order to work online. You may need to completely change your approach to deliver the same benefits online.

- Focus first on the quality of the experience—if there's value, people will pay.
- Innovate like an anthropologist. Watch what your members do, and adjust your approach.
- Encourage and listen to the input of members—they may have innovative ideas that you haven't thought of.
- Measure everything that matters, starting with retention.

20 From Ownership to Access

As I point out at the beginning of this book, much of our economy has operated historically on the principles of ownership. Companies manufacture and sell things; consumers and organizations *buy* them and then *own* them, taking on the rights and responsibilities of private ownership.

What's different about today's Membership Economy is that technology makes it possible for individuals to connect directly to products and services via cloud technology. Technology also allows customers to connect directly and continuously to the company itself. As a result, access models enable stronger relationships, greater loyalty, and more benefits for members.

As individuals grow frustrated with the responsibilities of owning too much stuff (think of the successful self-storage industry), they are looking for ways to cut back on ownership while simultaneously finding new ways to access the products and services they want.

> The transformation from ownership to access results in lower risk, lower up-front expenses, and lower maintenance.

It's the difference between owning a huge music collection of CDs and accessing the music in the cloud (Pandora, Spotify). It's the difference between buying a DVD and streaming (Netflix, Amazon). It's the difference between owning a car and sharing one for a quick shopping trip (RelayRides, Zip-Car). It's the difference between hosting your own software on your own computer and accessing it as a service (Adobe, Intuit, Salesforce).

To transition from an ownership model to a membership model, you need to start by taking a big step back. At the root of any good business are three things—vision, mission, and culture. The tree trunk is made strong by the enterprise's core competencies. The branches represent specific products and services. Management plays the role of arborists, tending to the tree, pruning back products and service offerings that are no longer healthy to allow others to thrive, and treating the tree with mulch, pesticides, and soil infusions to protect it from pesty competitors and the changing weather of market conditions. Look at the roots and trunk of your business and ask these fundamental questions:

- What is core to your business? Why does your business exist? What strengths have you built?
- What benefits do your customers get from the different branches of your business?
- What alternative products, services, or organizations also provide those benefits—even if they are not traditional competitors?
- What disadvantages do your current members complain about most?

For your members, the transformation from ownership to access should result in lower risk, lower up-front expenses, and lower maintenance. If it doesn't, they will leave. And some of them will leave—it's part of the pruning process. You might experience some additional, short-term revenue decline in transitioning from the big and lumpy transactions to small, recurring payments. That's all right. If you've structured the transition properly, the business lost will be made up many times over in business gained. Let's examine the experiences of Adobe, Intuit, and Amazon, three companies that have moved from ownership to access.

Adobe: Transitioning Successfully from Offline to Online

The story of Adobe's transition from ownership to membership garnered a lot of press attention, some of it negative. But it is actually an example of a pretty successful case.

In May 2013, Adobe changed its model from licensing Adobe's Creative Suite Software, sold as a physical disk, to a cloud-based subscription to Adobe's Creative Cloud. Creative Cloud grants access to software, as well as some new features with respect to sharing.

By November 2013, Adobe had reached 1.44 million Creative Cloud customers, sending its stock to an all-time high. Despite all the sign-ups, which were arriving faster than Adobe initially predicted, lots of long-time customers were displeased with Adobe's move. They didn't like the idea of software that stops working if they stop paying, leaving projects high and dry unless they resubscribe. Disgruntled customers called upon Adobe to rethink its discontinuation of the boxed software, but Adobe is sticking with subscriptions. As we have discussed, anytime you force members to change, there will be fallout. But sometimes it's worth the cost. Despite the complaints, most of those who signed up plan to renew, according to a 2014 survey from CNET and analyst firm Jeffries.[1]

Compare this story with that of Weight Watchers Online. Weight Watchers spun off its new business model, and gave consumers a choice to use offline, online, or a hybrid. Adobe didn't provide a choice. It just ripped off the BandAid with a big "Ta-da!" And it suffered some bad reviews. But ultimately Adobe has thrived. Adobe's approach was certainly riskier but it was also less expensive and more decisive. Adobe didn't commit to maintaining multiple options for its customers. Adobe might have had a smoother transition if it had continued to support the ownership model as well as the membership model. On the other hand, making such a clear change has made it easier for Adobe to move the company aggressively toward more of a relationship-driven approach with customers.

Intuit: Transition from CD Ownership to Subscription Access

Like Adobe, Intuit initially established its customer base by selling packaged desktop programs. QuickBooks, its popular accounting software application, lets small businesses create and manage invoices, pay bills, prepare tax forms, and handle payroll.

A marketing-oriented company, Intuit noted changing demands from customers. It also recognized the possibilities of newly available technologies. CEO Brad Smith noticed that many businesses were moving to subscription models, which provided three key sources of ongoing value to users:

- *Access from anywhere,* via any computer, and by multiple users—key in a company with multiple employees.
- *Access to the very best, latest features and services,* without having to constantly shop for the newest offering.
- *Connection with the company* for faster, more insightful service than was possible with a traditional call center.

Intuit also saw that a move to an access model could be good for the company:

- *Cloud* for data
- *Network effect of developers,* creating and improving product
- *Network effect of users,* building ties to one another, reinforcing engagement and loyalty
- *Recurring revenue model,* which drives a much higher valuation

Smith has said that the key issue in the online business "is converting first-time users into second-time and ongoing users," which he recognized was a big transition for a packaged software company.[3]

In 2000, Intuit began offering Quick-Books Online.[4] Many customers switched as soon as QuickBooks for the Web became

> *Customers loved the low initial cost, the constantly updated features, and the ability to connect remotely with employees.*

available. Customers loved the low initial cost, the constantly updated features, and the ability to connect remotely with employees. And for a while, with both offerings available, everyone was happy. However, over time Intuit discontinued its fixed price offering. Customers were frustrated with this mandatory change, and there was a minority that didn't benefit from the new features and offerings. These frustrations caused a lot of problems for Intuit as many customers felt that the new membership model provided less value, often at a higher total cost of ownership.

For example, a small business with simple invoicing processes and only one person managing all accounting did not need the multiple points of access, the additional functionality, and the constant updates. So such businesses were frustrated with the mandatory change, just as some of Adobe's customers were. Even with the gradual transition from ownership to access, Intuit still lost some customers.

Intuit's transition from ownership to access has been slow and careful, with support for both approaches. In addition, it has experimented with attractive promotions to convert packaged software users into what Smith calls "connected services customers." Perhaps the company has been too slow, as other subscription and community accounting companies have had time to establish themselves and steal market share. Intuit has received some criticism for its slow transition, but it looks like its new model is working—it reports a new QuickBooks for the Web subscriber on average every minute of every day.[5] For Intuit, a slower approach worked better than a big forced change. Transparency about the change, communicated clearly to its customers, combined with extensive planning and analysis, helped the transition succeed.

Key Considerations in Moving from Ownership to Access—Initial Transition

When an organization moves from ownership to access, leaders need to consider three key issues at the outset.

1. *Product.* Rebuild the product so that it can be offered as a subscription, not a transaction—access and not ownership. This often involves starting from scratch. For tech companies, it implies a new infrastructure. For offline organizations, it might require access to support, always-current data, or shared pools of resources with a library model. The important thing is that the new offering is at parity, or ideally, even better than the prior offering, and that the benefits will help customers in the long term, if not also in the short term.

2. *Pricing.* Rethink pricing—what is the value of access for a finite period of time? A month? A year? Will existing customers have the new standard pricing, or will they have a special "grandfathered" arrangement that recognizes and rewards them for their loyalty?

3. *Communication.* Communicate the changes to existing customers. Be as transparent as possible. If there are advantages in the short term, explain them. If there are only longer-term advantages but the transition won't immediately result in benefits, be honest. Transitioning from ownership to access has implications in terms of the kind of relationship you will have with your customers— they will become members and will expect a real relationship that lasts. So start clean and with integrity.

Amazon: Weaving Membership into Its Model

Unlike Intuit and Adobe, both software manufacturers, Amazon is a retailer transitioning from a traditional transactional model to one that leverages the principles of membership. While Amazon is still at heart a retailer, it has experimented in small and big ways with new models of membership.

Online retailing giant Amazon has been groundbreaking in its investment in membership. Starting as an online retailer of books, the company evolved into a retailer of everything, then a technology platform for all kinds of retailers, a hardware company, and a digital source of content and services. Other companies could learn a lot from Amazon—most importantly the value of constant innovation and investment.

> *Membership and community are related and overlap, but they aren't the same. Amazon has invested in building both.*

Amazon has tested different flavors of community and membership over the years. Membership and community are related and overlap, but they aren't the same. Membership, as we've discussed, is about a formal, ongoing relationship between organization and member. Community is about connection and communication among a group of people with shared interests. Amazon has invested in building both. Three of the most successful examples are Amazon Prime, Amazon Forums, and Woot.

Amazon Prime is a paid membership program. Amazon's approach has been to have members pay something so that they are more invested. Payment and commitment change members' emotional and psychological attitudes and behavior. Prime is intentionally "premium" as a means of establishing itself as something special. Amazon has systematically and thoughtfully continued to invest in layering benefits over the core offering of "free two-day shipping" (and it's working on same-day delivery).

Additional benefits, which are costly for Amazon to deliver, include access to lots of digital benefits, such as the Kindle Lending Library, Amazon Prime Instant Video, and Amazon Prime Music. Amazon is trying to build loyalty and create behaviors around how its members engage with the company.

I'm not sure if Prime members feel a sense of community. But loyalty manifests itself in their behavior.

Amazon Forums are free communities. Amazon has tried a number of different tactics on the nonpaid side over the years, in addition to paid Prime. One active example is Amazon's forums section. Amazon has dozens of forums. Some, like the "Michael Jackson" forum, are incredibly active. It's obvious that some people spend a lot of time writing their point of view, responding to other points of views, and answering questions. Many of them are fanatical reviewers—some with more than 500 posted reviews. These reviewers will often post every night at 12:01 to review newly released products and deals of the day. Top reviewers compete for pride of place, mostly for the social benefit and status. Generally, they are not professional reviewers.

Woot is a "deal a day" site that Amazon acquired in 2010.[6] Known for its quirky vibe and devoted community, Woot is a place where Amazon can explore community and membership. Community members comment on the quality of deals, pointing out better deals available elsewhere or encouraging others to act on an especially good deal. Some members just post for fun, to amuse other community members. The fun community is key to the success of the site.

Why is Amazon investing in so many experiments in membership? I think it's because it sees the huge potential in building lasting, ongoing relationships and transforming its customers into members. Its attention to research into all market segments has given it a foundation on which to build both community and membership.

What Can We Learn from This Model?

Technology has enabled many kinds of business models to embrace membership. And many are transitioning. While this model can be beneficial for both the organization and the customer, not everyone emerges victorious. For the ones who don't want to change, a new business model can be frustrating or feel unfair.

The best organizations continue to innovate on their business model. They want to move beyond competitive one-upmanship to find green field opportunities to continue to impress and delight customers—and membership is a way to differentiate from the competition. However, they need to be careful to provide ongoing, evolving value that justifies the ongoing costs. They also need to be sure that they make the transition in a way that doesn't create resentment among loyal customers.

Adobe could have made its transition from ownership to access less traumatic than it did, but it seems to have survived the tempest. Intuit has been making its QuickBooks transition slowly and carefully. And Amazon continues to experiment with and invest in one innovation after another. Each of these solutions can work.

Remember

- Offer additional value to justify the ongoing costs of membership.
- Consider supporting the ownership model, at least for any subsets of loyal owners for whom your new access model doesn't make sense, even if you transition everyone else to an access model.
- Be transparent about change; communicate clearly to stakeholders who include customers, employees, vendors, and shareholders.
- Research and analyze impact across all market segments.
- Expect push-back if you're forcing customers into a new model and be prepared to respond.

21

From Business as Usual to Competitive Disruption

When Harvard business professor Clayton Christensen published *The Innovator's Dilemma* in 1997, he put companies on notice. Christensen argued that well-run businesses aren't immune—in fact, it's their strong processes that put them at risk. He asserted that "good business practices can, nevertheless, weaken a great firm."[1] Even "companies that had their competitive antennae up, listened astutely to customers and invested aggressively in new technologies still lost their market dominance." What can happen is competitive disruption.

Successful companies often feel blindsided by competition. In the context of the Membership Economy, an organization that does not truly operate with the members' needs at the center of the business model can be especially vulnerable when someone comes in with a radically new approach that meets the members' needs better than, faster than, and/or cheaper than existing options.

Longtime leaders are sometimes tempted to fill holes rather than build mountains. They quickly copy the disruptor, filling in gaps in their existing offerings instead of planning a major response using the organization's resources, contacts, and reputation to create something new and special, something that inspires people (customers, employees, investors) to rally around. Speed is good, but sometimes it's not enough.

The Membership Economy takes advantage of new technologies that enable less expensive and more predictable models for delivering value. As a result, membership-oriented organizations can move quickly to disrupt other organizations, even those that are part of the Membership Economy themselves. In this chapter, we look at two companies that have disrupted entire industries, LinkedIn and Airbnb. LinkedIn's tremendous success has impacted many industries, even professional associations, which are themselves membership organizations. Airbnb has taken aim at the hospitality industry, one which has had limited engagement in the Membership Economy, with the exception of its loyalty programs.

LinkedIn: Competitive Disruption Based on Benefits

LinkedIn is one of the scariest organizations posing a potential threat to professional associations. As of May 2014, LinkedIn had over 300 million members, according to research by eMarketer in 2013,[2] 40 percent of those members check their account at least once a day.[3] LinkedIn is creating a supercommunity of professionals. It offers all professionals free membership and provides many benefits similar to those of professional associations, including:

- A contact network consisting of name and location.
- Members can find jobs, people, and opportunities recommended by their contacts.
- Employers can list jobs for potential candidates.
- Job seekers can review the profile of hiring managers and discover which of their contacts can make an introduction.
- Members can post photos and view photos of others to aid in identification.

- Members can follow different companies and receive notifications about new members and offers.
- Members can save (bookmark) jobs of interest.
- Members can "like" and "congratulate" other users based on their status updates, thus building relationships.
- Journalists can reach out to experts directly without sourcing them through professional societies.
- Members can see who visited their profile page.
- Members can join discussion "circles" focused on professional interests and easily invite others to join the conversation.
- Members create their own interest groups under the LinkedIn umbrella. In other words, the LinkedIn "groups" provide features similar to membership associations.
- Members can ask the group questions and enjoy real-time feedback.

> *Private sector companies like LinkedIn can serve many of the functions of professional associations, often better than the associations can themselves.*

Here's an example of how LinkedIn is changing the way individuals engage with their professional associations, and why the associations are worried. The Association of Personal Historians (personalhistorians .org) has been struggling to increase membership for years. According to the association's president, Sarah White, its membership growth has been relatively flat since 2008, and hasn't been able to break through 650 members and reach 700, its next goal. Meanwhile, its LinkedIn group has grown from 0 to 1,000 in the same period.[4]

When I give talks to professional groups, I always ask how many are on LinkedIn. A few years ago, just a fraction of the members of the audience—maybe a quarter—raised their hands. But by 2014, 90 to 95 percent raise their hands. LinkedIn has become a giant listing of every professional who works, complete with résumés.

LinkedIn has also been able to create company profiles. It can tell you how many people a company has hired in the last six months and for which titles. If you see that of those 14 hires, half of them have the word "international" in their titles, you can surmise that the business is going global. These data are valuable and make a lot of the benefits of professional associations obsolete.

Private sector companies like LinkedIn can serve many of the functions of professional associations, often better than the associations can themselves. Many associations are struggling with these challenges. They have long histories, large memberships, and decent budgets. They enjoy the benefits of strong brands and clear missions. But they have struggled to keep up with technology and win in the Membership Economy. If they aren't delivering on the promise of the mission, members will look elsewhere. And right now, many members want faster, easier ways to connect, stay current, and impact the future. The opportunity is there for the nonprofits to thrive, but only if they focus on continuous innovation and attracting new members as opposed to just serving the past.

Allen Blue, LinkedIn's cofounder, is one of the true experts on digital membership. Blue's insights are particularly useful for professional association CEOs but are also relevant for Membership Economy organizations of all types.

Blue starts from the basic premise that there's every reason to believe that the online systems are a shorter path to the same value. "If you focus on technology as enabling new ways of delivering value that people need, as opposed to just being a benefit unto itself, you can apply the technology to make things easier and faster. As a result of technology, all kinds of non-physically dependent communities have emerged, providing faster, cheaper ways to discover new contacts and stay connected with people we already know. Since we have more choices, we expect organizations to make it clear why four meetings a year or a weekly gathering at the local pizza place is worth the investment of time plus money."[5]

The solution for the longtime organization, says Blue, is to go back to the core mission. Membership associations need to understand what their members are lacking and find differentiated ways to serve them—and to package the value. Blue suggested that these longtime membership organizations consider temporarily setting aside legacy programs in order to reimagine what their membership would really want.

This entrepreneurial lens could be what organizations need to be able to think creatively about how to stay relevant and build on existing strengths to maintain longtime relationships and brand.

LinkedIn may not have been founded with the objective of disrupting executive recruiting, formal networking groups, and professional associations, but that's been its effect. In contrast, Airbnb set out deliberately to disrupt the hospitality industry—and it has been successful in doing that.

Airbnb: Competitive Disruption Based on Community

Airbnb is often held up as an example of a new business model that is disrupting an entire industry—in this case, the hospitality industry. The company has unlocked the stored value in people's homes—rooms they don't need and that can be rented out to travelers. Homeowners get additional revenue. Travelers get a more affordable sleeping option. Everyone wins (except hotels and motels and city treasuries that need room-tax revenue).

> *Travelers get a more authentic, connected experience, and homeowners have the opportunity to open their homes to new acquaintances.*

But Airbnb is about more than cheap room rentals. Airbnb is creating community and belonging. Travelers get a more authentic, connected experience, and homeowners have the opportunity to open their homes to new acquaintances. Both build relationships with people they otherwise might never meet.

The idea of belonging and building community is critical to Airbnb. In fact, the company has created a word and a logo to describe this new kind of belonging: Bélo. When the company launched its new logo, it posted on its blog: "However we first entered this community, we all know that getting in isn't a transaction. It's a connection that can last a lifetime. That's because the rewards you get from Airbnb aren't just financial—they're personal—for hosts and guests alike. At a time when new technologies have made it easier to keep each other at a distance, you're using them to bring people together. And you're tapping into the universal human yearning to belong—the desire to feel welcomed, respected and appreciated for who you are, no matter where you might be."[6]

What is revolutionary about Airbnb's business model is that it's not transactional; it's about belonging, and it taps into a deep human need, a message that resonates with consumers. While staying in a stranger's home isn't going to be everyone's ideal travel experience, the lower prices, combined with increased human connection, have Airbnb growing at a rapid pace.

According to a March 2014 *Fast Company* article, the current rate of Airbnb's expansion, which boasts 550,000 listings in 192 countries, will soon surpass the InterContinental Hotels Group and Hilton Worldwide as the world's largest hotel chain. Founder Brian Chesky has said that he wants to transform Airbnb into a full-blown hospitality brand and has indicated that he "sees an opportunity to democratize a lot of the services that the Four Seasons provides." Right now, hotel operators are putting on a brave face, saying that Airbnb could never provide the same experience they do and that they are doing fine.[7] But to me, the hotels sound a lot like Barnes & Noble, circa 2009.

Disruption Happens, Even in the Membership Economy

What disrupts businesses today are the same things that have always disrupted businesses. It's just that the changes in economics and the rise of new entrants have put even the most established organizations at risk. Membership organizations themselves can be disrupted. And because they often have automated recurring revenue models, changes in consumer behavior often become evident only gradually, making it easy for management to miss the changing landscape.

If benefits aren't unique but rather a "bundle" of stuff that's available elsewhere, the organization has a problem. This happens when a newspaper offers a free T-shirt or a museum offers a bundled discount at the store, reciprocal membership, and a museum mug. The benefits are likely irrelevant to the member who wants to engage with the organization for the long term and may attract the wrong kind of member—the kind who just wants a free mug. (Do you really want the member who joins for a free mug?)

I was recently talking to a client firm that was moving from an advertising-based publishing model to a subscription model. Its approach was to throw in all of their content, plus some e-books from their partner (also available for free on the partner's site), plus some leftover logo wear from a prior event.

> *In many cases, it's not the stuff people want, it's the curation and community.*

What it didn't do was focus in on the subsegment of people who were interested in a subscription. It didn't take the time to analyze what benefits these people would love, and what they could get elsewhere. All the benefits the organization offered were simply combinations of free and inexpensive products and benefits that the organization could easily and cost-effectively provide, not what its members actually wanted.

Many content-oriented companies try this approach of just gathering as much content as possible and offering it at a monthly price when their members might want depth in a few key areas or access to a community of like-minded people. In many cases, it's not the *stuff* people want; it's the curation and community.

If the primary benefit is supposed to be the community, there must be a critical mass to enable a network effect. This means that the group itself and the connections of members to one another is the primary benefit of joining the community.

Many entrepreneurs see the demand for specialized communities— parents, families, certain types of professionals, hobbyists, even specific groups looking for love—and try to establish online communities for them. These kinds of membership organizations are built around the network effect. Once such a group is established (think Facebook, LinkedIn, or Match.com), the membership organization does not have to invest a lot to support the community—even without new content, features, or physical benefits, the community itself is valuable.

By looking at the challenges faced by companies like Mixx and Napster as well as the disruptive innovations that turned news, music, books, and hospitality upside down, what have we learned? Even the biggest, most solid industries can crumble when competitors begin to eat away at their business models.

What Can We Learn from This Model?

If an enterprise has been successful, its leaders tend to feel that what worked yesterday will work tomorrow. When all is going well, it's difficult to imagine that some tiny up-start can disrupt your business and remake your industry. Yet as former Intel CEO Andy Grove said, "Only the paranoid survive." And Dawn Sweeney, CEO of the National Restaurant Association, asks her team every few months: "If you wanted to put us out of business, what would you do?"

Perhaps the best way to avoid being disrupted is to stay as close to your members as possible. The more loyal members feel toward the company, the association, the museum, the store, the more difficult it is for a competitor to take them away. Combined with proactive evaluation of new enabling technologies and business models, keeping members at the core of your model can keep you in business regardless of new entrants.

Remember

- Three key drivers of disruption in the Membership Economy are:
  - *The Membership Economy principles themselves.* In general, taking a nonmembership model and thinking about how to apply Membership Economy principles can lead to disruptive innovation.

- *Accessing stored value.* Stored value in the form of underutilized assets can drive disruptive membership models.
- *New technology.* New technology developments can set the stage for disruption—organizations should leapfrog with each major new technological advance rather than wait for new entrants to step in.

■ Organizations that pass on legacy expenses to members run a risk of being beaten by new organizations that don't have the baggage.

■ As an organization grows, it becomes more likely to be a target, moving from disruptor to disruptee.

Conclusion: How You Can Start Transitioning Today

Congratulations. You've made it to the last chapter of the book. You're ready to apply the best practices of the Membership Economy. You want to make some changes that will help you and your organization to better achieve your goals.

"What's next?" you ask.

In their great book *The Knowing-Doing Gap* [Harvard Business School Press, 2000], Stanford professors Jeff Pfeffer and Bob Sutton suggest that analysis must inspire action. I want to inspire you to take action—small, medium, or large. And I'd like to help you to begin as soon as you finish reading.

Before you begin riding off in all directions at once, however, I want to provide a few more tools to ensure that you are successful on your journey. In this chapter, I share some suggestions about how to take what you've learned and start applying it immediately. I start with some things you should do right now, and I then provide some more general suggestions for each of the types of companies we've discussed.

What Should You Do Right Now?

You should start by putting down this book and picking up a pen. Give yourself time to reflect on what you've learned. Here are 10 questions to get you started. Just answer each one quickly, without worrying too much about the details.

1. What attracted you to the idea of the Membership Economy? What resonates with you?
2. Is there a particular organization you think can benefit from the Membership Economy? Maybe the place where you work or maybe a nonprofit that is close to your heart?
3. Which of the strategies discussed in Section II appeals to you most?
4. Which of the organization types described in Section III is most like yours?
5. Was there a particular example that grabbed your attention? Why?
6. Are you at a point of inflection—do you have an opportunity to scale a new mountain and transform your organization?
7. If a disruptor stole your best members, how would it do it? What would be the value proposition that would entice them away despite their deep loyalty?
8. Who on your team can help you think through the opportunities you have to leverage the power of the Membership Economy?
9. What other resources, skills, and experiences would help you make the changes you want to make? Are there people you know who could help you, as mentors, peers, or paid advisors?
10. What, if anything, is stopping you from making some small changes now? How can you clear those roadblocks?

Once you've had a chance to think for a while, reach out to your colleagues—just a few, no more than three. It's hard to innovate by consensus. If they're already familiar with the language of the

Membership Economy, great, but it's not necessary. Just get them in a room and say, "I have some ideas that I'd like to get your feedback on," and start sharing.

Set a goal of finding one or two opportunities for small tests. Pick something manageable but something that could have big implications if it works. Choose something that you're drawn to. It doesn't matter where you start, so start someplace that is exciting to you and feels big and easy. Assign action items: Start gathering data, mapping out changes, building support. Agree to meet in two days to see where you are. Don't let too much time lapse because you're trying to build momentum!

Take a look at the discussion on onboarding in Chapter 6. How can you build engagement and support to make the changes you wish to make? Make it fun. Reward people for their contributions. This meeting should feel creative and exciting—not like work.

Any organization could start in virtually any place, with any number of case studies, strategies, and goals as inspiration. However, there are some tactics that seem to be particularly effective for certain types of organizations. Following are a few specific suggestions.

Suggestions for Your Kind of Organization?

The following suggestions are actions for owners and managers of different types of membership organizations. Don't feel you have to stick with the label that defines your organization. I encourage you to seek to find lessons from each. But I've found that certain types of organizations often have similar challenges and opportunities, and I am trying to pinpoint some of those here.

I sincerely hope you give some of these strategies a try—and let me know how they work out!

Online Subscription Models
If you run a subscription business, the most important thing is to make sure the model works before investing in awareness. If you're

just starting out, it's worthwhile to figure this out before you launch. If you're already in operation, you need to make sure your offering/ benefits/members still align well. Here are some key things to ask yourself right now:

- Does your value proposition speak to your target buyers?
- Are your members willing to pay for your services "forever"?
- Does your sign-up flow and onboarding process work, or are you suffering from too many leaks in your funnel?
- Are you 100 percent sure your members will be loyal before you invest in acquisition?
- Do you have both short-term and long-term business strategies that work together?

> Make sure your members will be loyal before you invest in acquisition.

When you're just starting out, try to stick with a single offering because it's less confusing and leaves room to adjust price in the future. Remember, strong subscription businesses must have very high retention rates. If you don't, fix this before you invest further in marketing. On the other hand, make sure new members keep joining, because acquisition is proof that your offer continues to be relevant. Never confuse inertia with loyalty.

I'd also look at how the most active and loyal members (probably two different groups) are using the community and build features around them, maybe for a subscription. I'd also look at the data the organization collects and see what kind of value there is in the aggregated data— maybe it can be sold or built into another service.

Online Communities

If you're just getting started, the trickiest thing can be building enough value to attract the first member. If this is your challenge, I suggest you consider three options:

- Start with a smaller-focused value proposition. When LinkedIn started, the benefit of having your résumé online in a public place was valuable enough to make the (free) effort to post it. Critical mass of members and the related benefits came later.
- Do a partnership deal to get a critical mass of members, ideally a group of like-minded people who have built-in reasons to trust and help one another.
- Seed your membership organization with highly motivated, active participants—even if you have to pay them.

On the other hand, if you've already built a big community, chances are that you're now more focused on how to make money from the community. One place to start is by seeing what your most active users are asking for in the product. The requests from these engaged users can lead to new pricing tiers. Strong communities and social networks usually need help with monetization. I'd encourage you to think about what additional value these edge-case users need—they'd most likely be willing to pay for new services.

Loyalty Programs

If you run a loyalty program, my big question is: How can you incorporate loyalty into your whole business model—not just as a marketing program? Can you build support in your organization for a more differentiated experience for your members?

Even if your colleagues aren't on board yet, I'd suggest you focus on providing access to unique experiences for your best members rather than on financial benefits only. The best things money can't buy. Can you take members someplace special? Give them access to people they wouldn't otherwise meet? Remove friction from the generally stressful travel process?

Or, if you're feeling really ambitious, I'd suggest you blow up your program and start over. What does it mean to be loyal? What behavior do you want to reward? What would it look like if you really rewarded loyalty? What rewards truly generate a virtuous cycle of loyalty? And can you design a unique program that wouldn't work for your competitors— or for any other organization—because it comes out of your unique capabilities? Use the data you're collecting to track behavior, improve your offering, and avoid surprise cancellations.

Too many loyalty programs are commodities, effectively just discounts for volume purchases, and don't really create authentic loyalty or strengthen membership relationships. Don't be that kind of loyalty program. You have an opportunity to build something special!

Traditional Membership Economy Companies

If you told me you were already a successful membership-oriented company, I'd ask you to consider your mission from scratch to be sure you are still delivering value in the best way possible with today's technology.

> Invite your team members to brainstorm about how they'd crush your company.

Technology has changed dramatically in the past 20 years, and most organizations that predate these advances have not adapted to the changes as fully as the digital natives have. While changing the culture of an entire organization can be difficult, an easier way to bring in the digital native's comfort with technology is through acquisitions of start-ups and creation of independent "skunkworks" tasked with identifying opportunities for radical innovation. Invite your team members to brainstorm about how they'd crush your company, and see if you can identify some small experiments with radical intent to quickly test the most potentially impactful ideas.

I'd also encourage you to invest in continuous improvement.

Small Businesses and Consultancies

If you run a small business, you have a big opportunity. You probably already know your best customers, personally. What are the challenges that bring them to you? How can you help them beyond what you're doing today? Think about whether there are ways that you can build community among your customers with you at the center.

Can you take advantage of your size to provide a more customized experience than the big guys can? For the restaurant near my house, it means storing and serving its members' wine collections. For independent consultants it means that the work is being done by the owner, not the most junior person—clients want that kind of access. Give them more!

For small business membership organizations, the key is focus, exclusivity, and recognition. People want to be known and appreciated for what is unique. Small businesses are set up to recognize the individual's needs and build community better than any other type of organization.

Nonprofits, Professional Societies, and Trade Associations

Associations and nonprofits like churches, museums, and unions are among the longest-standing of the membership organizations. Your strength is your weakness—you've been around a long time, and you're generally governed by your members. This means that you have really loyal members who may be driving you in a direction that isn't attracting new blood.

When was the last time you considered changing your offerings, key fund-raisers, or membership programs? Do you think if you were starting from scratch, creating a new organization aimed to achieve your mission, that you'd come up with the same offerings? Brainstorm about what a start-up would do if it wanted to put you out of business. This is the same advice I give to traditional Membership Economy companies, because the two models have a lot of the same challenges.

I'd next suggest that you look at cash-strapped start-ups as role models. That's the other place where you might find inspiration. Many nonprofits and associations blame tight budgets and lack of access to growth capital for their challenges with innovation, but sometimes the issue is more about focus and resourcefulness. An advantage you might have is more data and access to members than most other organizations, so use these to keep a finger on the pulse of your members. Looking at how organizations like SurveyMonkey, the Lakewood Church, or CrossFit got off the ground can be very helpful.

Finally, I know you often face a challenge with governance. Because there isn't an "owner," whose profits determine success, nonprofits should be measured against the stated mission. Make sure you have a clear vision for achieving the mission and a well-structured action plan with milestones. The role of the governing bodies—boards and committees—is to make sure that you have a clear plan. The only card a governing body should have to play is the "fire the CEO" card. As long as you focus on objective metrics that measure progress against the stated mission, you're way more likely to build support with the board.

Final Words

No matter what kind of organization you're associated with, stay hungry. Keep innovating. Keep testing your assumptions. Keep questioning. Keep looking at macrotrends. Most importantly, look outside yourself. Find people who can go on this journey with you. Maybe they're inside your organization, and you are lucky to have like-minded colleagues. But if you don't have colleagues, and maybe even if you do, look for mentors, peers, and kindred spirits who believe in membership and can work side-by-side with you, even if not for the same organization.

One of the biggest challenges I have faced after reading business books is the huge gap between what I've read and how to apply it. Sometimes I feel like the author has abandoned me right when I need help most. I want to be there for each of you if I can. So I'll leave you with an offer. If, after reading this book, you want to incorporate the Membership Economy into your organization, let me know. I'm building an online community to support the Membership Economy, but in the meantime, just send me an email to rbaxter@peninsulastrategies.com with your specific question, and I'll do my best to answer it. Best of luck, and please keep in touch!

Glossary

To help clarify some of the terms in the book, here's a brief glossary.

acquisition funnel: Also referred to as *conversion funnel* or *demand funnel*, this phrase refers to the customers' journey from the moment of awareness to the moment they become a customer. Many organizations use the idea of an acquisition funnel to track how well their marketing activities are working to attract and engage prospects.

consumerization of the enterprise: A sales strategy to build relationships with individual employees until reaching critical mass and then reaching out to establish a relationship with the enterprise itself.

evangelists: Members who feel so strongly about products and services that they freely convince others to try to buy them. Sometimes they are also superusers, but their engagement is targeted around encouraging new members.

free trial: An opportunity for prospects to sample the full benefits of a product or service for a finite period of time without paying. Unlike the freemium, free trials last for a finite period.

freemium: A feature in a subscription business model in which members can choose from either a free option that provides ongoing value (forever) or any number of paid subscription options. (free + premium = freemium.)

friction: Anything that slows people down when they are trying to engage with the membership or organization. For example, a complicated sign-up process or confusing instructions might cause friction.

gamification: Applying game thinking and mechanics to nongame settings, usually as a motivator to encourage a certain type of behavior.

hourglass funnel: A specific kind of funnel that tracks a customer's journey from the moment of awareness through the point of becoming a customer, but then continues on, tracking the customer's impact on revenue through referrals and additional purchases.

network effect: A situation in which each additional member drives value for all existing members just by joining. For example, Skype is more valuable to the hundredth person who joins than the first person. After all, who could that first person Skype with before anyone else joined?

onboarding: The process of getting a new member fully engaged in the membership. The term is also used to describe the process of acclimating new employees to the organization.

paywall: An online feature that prevents users from accessing specific options or features without paying a higher price. Paywalls encourage users to upgrade their membership to gain access to greater value.

pricing tiers: Different payment options for a subscription service. As the value increases through added features, volume, and service, the subscription rate rises. Most subscription models have multiple pricing tiers.

sharing economy: Also referred to as the *peer-to-peer economy* or *collaborative consumption*, it's a business model that is built around sharing assets. Unlike traditional models, consumers and not the organization maintain ownership of the assets. Examples include Airbnb and RelayRides.

software as a service (SaaS): A software licensing and delivery model in which the vendor licenses software on a subscription basis. The software is centrally hosted in the cloud. Examples are QuickBooks, Salesforce, Egnyte, and Marketo.

stickiness: Elements of an online experience that encourage the user to stay longer. Critical element in retention.

subscription: Customers pay a periodic fee for access to services, content, or even physical products. Contrasts with ownership transactions.

superusers: Those especially loyal and engaged members who leverage the power of the community through their participation. Superusers are members who spend a significant amount of time participating in the community.

switching costs: The costs incurred by customers when they change from one solution to a substitute.

viral: Types of marketing tactics that achieve goals through self-replicating viral processes, similar to the spread of biological or computer viruses. The first widely used example of viral marketing was hotmail, in which each email sent had an offer inviting the email recipient to sign up for the hotmail service.

NOTES

SECTION I

Chapter 1

1. Robert Putnam, *Bowling Alone: The Collapse and Revival of American Community* (New York: Touchstone Books, 2001) (http://bowlingalone.com).
2. Vindu Goel, "G.M. Uses Social Media to Manage Customers and Its Reputation," *New York Times*, March 24, 2014, accessed September 7, 2014, http://www.nytimes.com/2014/03/24/business/after-huge-recall-gm-speaks-to-customers-through-social-media.html?_r=0.
3. Emily Steel, "'Ice Bucket Challenge' Has Raised Millions for ALS Association," *New York Times*, August 17, 2014, accessed August 24, 2014, http://www.nytimes.com/2014/08/18/business/ice-bucket-challenge-has-raised-millions-for-als-association.html.

Chapter 2

1. "About IMVU," accessed August 26, 2014, http://www.imvu.com/about/.
2. Conversation with Cary Rozenzweig, May 22, 2014.

Chapter 3

1. Gail Sullivan, "Facebook Responds to Criticism of Its Experiment on Users," *Washington Post*, June 30, 2014, accessed August 25, 2014, http://www.washingtonpost.com/news/morning-mix/wp/2014/06/30/facebook-responds-to-criticism-of-study-that-manipulated-users-news-feeds/.

SECTION II

Chapter 4

1. Conversation with Kevin Donnellan and Lynn Mento, October 22, 2014.
2. (Time McDonald).

Chapter 6

1. Conversation with Camille Watson, May 30, 2014.
2. Lithium website, accessed August 26, 2014, http://www.lithium.com/company/.
3. Conversation with Michael Wu, May 23, 2014.
4. Michael Wu, "The 90-9-1 Rule in Reality," *Science of Social Blog*, September 14, 2012, accessed August 26, 2014, http://community.lithium.com/t5/Science-of-Social-blog/The-90-9-1-Rule-in-Reality/ba-p/5463.
5. Conversation with Jimi Letchford, October 30, 2014.

6. Katie Steinmetz, "Here's What Happened When I Tried a Children's Weight-Loss App," *Time*, July 29, 2014, accessed August 21, 2014. https://kurbo.com/.
7. Conversation with Dawn Sweeney, August 1, 2014.
8. Conversation with Chris McGill, May 30, 2014.

Chapter 8
1. John Borland, "Napster Reaches Settlement with Publishers," CNET, September 24, 2001, accessed September 2, 2014, http://news.cnet.com/2100-1023-273394.html.
2. Julianne Pepitone, "Today Is Napster's Last Day of Existence," CNN, November 30, 2011, accessed September 2, 2014, http://money.cnn.com/2011/11/30/technology/napster_rhapsody.

Chapter 9
1. Conversation with Allen Blue, June 16, 2014.
2. Conversation with Michael Geller, August 4, 2014.
3. Conversation with Tien Tzuo, July 24, 2014.
4. Conversation with David Werdiger, June 18, 2014.
5. Conversation with Jamie Beckland, August 4, 2014.

Chapter 10
1. "Vine Your Disney Side," accessed September 4, 2014, http://disneysidecontest.com.
2. Conversation with Gene Hoffman, July 2, 2014.
3. Conversation with Gene Hoffman, July 2, 2014.

SECTION III
1. Verónica Maria Jarski, "Surprising Facts About Customer Loyalty Marketing," August 6, 2013, accessed August 26, 2014, http://www.marketingprofs.com/chirp/2013/11338/surprising-facts-about-customer-loyalty-marketing-infographic.

Chapter 11
1. Adam Lashinsky, "Why SurveyMonkey Is Holding Off on an IPO," *Fortune*, January 17, 2013, accessed August 23, 2014, http://fortune.com/2013/01/17/why-surveymonkey-is-holding-off-on-an-ipo/.
2. Conversation with Tim Maly, June 17, 2014.
3. Conversation with Vineet Jain, August 23, 2014.
4. Susan Schena, "Tech Firm Egnyte Moves into New 30,000-Sq.-Ft. Headquarters in Mountain View," *Patch*, May 20, 2014, accessed August 26, 2014, http://patch.com/california/mountainview/tech-firm-egnyte-moves-into-new-30000sqft-headquarters-in-mountain-view#.
5. Arik Hesseldahl, "Egnyte Barges into Crowded Corporate Cloud Business," May 23, 2014, accessed August 26, 2014, http://recode.net/2014/05/23/egnyte-barges-into-crowded-corporate-cloud-business/.
6. Conversation with Vineet Jain, August 23, 2014.

Chapter 12
1. Conversation with Allen Blue, June 16, 2014.
2. "Match.com Fact Sheet 2014," accessed September 2, 2014, http://match.mediaroom.com/index.php?s=30440.

3. Conversation with Fran Maier, August 27, 2014.
4. Craig Smith, "By the Numbers: 100 Amazing LinkedIn Statistics," August 24, 2014, accessed September 2, 2014, http://expandedramblings.com/index.php/by-the-numbers-a-few-important-linkedin-stats.
5. Conversation with Joff Redfern, June 9, 2014.
6. Jon Swartz, "LinkedIn Reports Loss Despite 46% Jump in Revenue," *USA Today*, May 1, 2014, accessed August 26, 2014, http/www.usatoday.com/story/tech/2014/05/01/linkedin-results.
7. Conversation with Bob Baxley, August 17, 2014.
8. Cat Zakrzewski, "Women Use Pinterest, but They Don't Run It," *TechCrunch*, July 24, 2014, accessed August 26, 2014, http://techcrunch.com/2014/07/24/women-use-pinterest-but-they-dont-run-it.
9. "Top 7 Social Media Sites from January to June 2014," *StatCounter Global Stats*, accessed January 16, 2015, http://gs.statcounter.com/all-social_media-ww-monthly-201401-201406-bar.

Chapter 13

1. Verónica Maria Jarski, "Surprising Facts About Customer Loyalty Marketing [Infographic]," August 6, 2013, accessed August 26, 2014, http://www.marketingprofs.com/chirp/2013/11338/surprising-facts-about-customer-loyalty-marketing-infographic.
2. Cameron Graham, "Study: Why Customers Participate in Loyalty Programs," July 23, 2014, accessed August 26, 2014, http://technologyadvice.com/gamification/blog/why-customers-participate-loyalty-programs.
3. Howard Schultz, *Pour Your Heart Into It* (New York: Hyperion, 1999).
4. Ric Garrido, "Colloquy.com Estimates U.S. Consumers Loyalty Program Points Value," Boarding Area blog, May 7, 2014, accessed August 28, 2014, http://loyaltytraveler.boardingarea.com/2011/05/07/colloquy-com-estimates-u-s-consumers-loyalty-program-points-value/.
5. Michael Bush, "Why Harrah's Loyalty Effort Is Industry's Gold Standard," October 5, 2009, accessed August 26, 2014, http://adage.com/article/news/harrah-s-loyalty-program-industry-s-gold-standard/139424/.
6. Caesars Entertainment, 2012 Colloquy Loyalty Awards, December 13, 2013, accessed August 26, 2014, https://www.youtube.com/watch?v=RSSXf_etugw&feature=youtube.

Chapter 14

1. Conversation with Elizabeth Crosta, June 27, 2014.
2. Conversation with Lindsay Pedersen, June 13, 2014.
3. Conversation with Iniko Basilio, June 3, 2014.
4. T-Mobile U.S. First Quarter 2014 Earnings Release, T-Mobile U.S., May 1, 2014, accessed August 26, 2014, http://newsroom.t-mobile.com/news/t-mobile-us-reports-first-quarter-2014-results-and-best-ever-quarterly-performance-in-branded-postpaid-net-customer-additions.htm.

Chapter 15

1. Bonnie Eslinger, "Kepler's Enters New Era with Owner's Retirement," *San Jose Mercury News*, January, 31, 2012, accessed August 26, 2014, http://www.mercurynews.com/peninsula/ci_19855156?source=rss.

2. Some of Weiss's most popular books include *Getting Started in Consulting, Million Dollar Consulting, Money Talks: How to Make a Million as a Speaker* and *Value-Based Fees: How to Charge—and Get—What You're Worth*.
3. "Alan's Forums," http://www.alansforums.com.

Chapter 16

1. Jim Hammerand, "Ahni & Zoe (formerly Creative Memories) Is Shutting Down in U.S. and Canada," August 5, 2014, accessed August 27, 2014, http://www.bizjournals .com/twincities/news/2014/08/05/ahni-zoe-creative-memories-shutting-down.html.
2. Conversation with Cathi Nelson, July 7, 2014.
3. "Policies," accessed August 26, 2014, http://www.sierraclub.org/policy.
4. Conversation with Michelle Epstein, June 20, 2014.
5. Conversation with Michelle Epstein, June 20, 2014.
6. Peter Murray, "The Secret of Scale," *Stanford Social Innovation Review*, Fall 2013, accessed August 26, 2014, http://www.ssireview.org/articles/entry/the_secret_of_scale.

SECTION IV

Chapter 17

1. Conversation with Allen Blue, June 16, 2014.
2. Conversation with Alex Benn, May 15, 2014.
3. Katharine Kaplan, "Facemash Creator Survives Ad Board," *The Harvard Crimson*, November 19, 2003, accessed August 24, 2014, http://www.thecrimson.com/ article/2003/11/19/facemash-creator-survives-ad-board-the/.

Chapter 18

1. "About Pandora," accessed August 28, 2014, http://www.pandora.com/about.
2. Erick Schonfeld, "With 80 Million Users, Pandora Files to Go Public," *TechCrunch*, February 11, 2011, accessed August 28, 2014, http://techcrunch.com/2011/02/11/ pandora-files-to-go-public/.
3. Joan E. Solsman, "Like a Rolling Milestone: Pandora Hits 250M Registered Users," *CNET*, February 27, 2014, accessed August 27, 2014, http://www.cnet.com/news/ like-a-rolling-milestone-pandora-hits-250m-registered-users/.
4. Conversation with Tim Westergren, July 8, 2014.
5. Conversation with Leyla Seka, September 4, 2014.
6. Conversation with Leyla Seka, September 4, 2014.
7. "Salesforce.com Named World's Most Innovative Company by Forbes Magazine for a Record Fourth Consecutive Year," August 20, 2014, *PRNewswire*, accessed September 4, 2014, http://news.morningstar.com/all/pr-news-wire/20140820SF94598/salesforcecom-named-worlds-most-innovative-company-by-forbes-magazine-for-a-record-fourth-consecutive-year.aspx.

Chapter 19

1. Conversation with David Kirchhoff, June 19, 2014.
2. Matthew Denos, "A Weight Watchers Case Study: How Smart Marketing Pays Off," *MarketingProfs*, March 28, 2013, accessed August 27, 2014, http://www .marketingprofs.com/articles/2013/10422/a-weight-watchers-case-study-how-smart-marketing-pays-off.

3. Maisie McCabe, "News Corp Promotes Katie Vanneck-Smith to MD of Dow Jones," *Campaign Live*, June 25, 2013, accessed August 28, 2014, http://www .campaignlive.co.uk/news/1300539/.

4. Ben Somerset, "Market Leader Interview—Katie Vanneck-Smith, Chief Marketing Officer of News International (NI)," *Creative Brief Blog*, June 25, 2013, accessed August 28, 2014, http://www.creativebrief.com/blog/2013/06/25/market-leader-interview-%E2%80%93-katie-vanneck-smith-chief-marketing-officer-of-news-international-ni/.

5. Tien Tzuo, Zuora and Katie Vannek-Smith, "Digital Media and the Art of Engagement," *Wired.com*, July 14, 2014, accessed August 28, 2014, http:// innovationinsights.wired.com/insights/2014/07/digital-media-art-engagement/.

6. http://thebrainscoop.tumblr.com/post/51777406956/im-not-sure-that-excited-even-begins-to-cover-it.

Chapter 20

1. Stephen Shankland, "Despite Complaints, Most Adobe Creative Cloud Subscribers Plan to Renew," *CNET*, March 13, 2014, accessed August 28, 2014, http://www.cnet .com/news/despite-complaints-most-adobe-creative-cloud-subscribers-plan-to-renew/.

2. Conversation with John Kremer, October 17, 2014.

3. Fredric Paul, "Inside Intuit: How A Software Kingpin Is Remaking Itself for Mobile & Services," September 19, 2012, accessed August 28, 2014, http://readwrite .com/2012/09/19/inside-intuit-how-a-software-kingpin-is-remaking-itself-for-mobile-services.

4. Michael Liedtke, "Growth Spurt at Intuit," *Los Angeles Times*, August 26, 2002, accessed http://articles.latimes.com/2002/aug/26/business/fi-intuit26.

5. Hal Gregersen, "How Intuit Innovates by Challenging Itself," *HBR Blogs*, February 6, 2014, accessed August 28, 2014, http://blogs.hbr.org/2014/02/how-intuit-innovates-by-challenging-itself/.

6. M. G. Siegler, "Woot's Deal of the Day: Woot!—Amazon Buys It. Price? $110 Million," *TechCrunch*, June 30, 2010, accessed August 28, 2014, http:// techcrunch.com/2010/06/30/woot-amazon/.

Chapter 21

1. Clayton M. Christensen, *The Innovator's Dilemma: When New Technologies Cause Great Firms to Fail*, Cambridge, MA: Harvard Business Press (1997), http://books .google.com/books/about/?id=SIexi_qgq2gC.

2. "About LinkedIn," 2014, accessed August 31, 2014, http://press.linkedin.com/about.

3. "Social Usage Involves More Platforms, More Often," July 2, 2013, accessed September 2, 2014, http://www.emarketer.com/Article/Social-Usage-Involves-More-Platforms-More-Often/1010019.

4. Conversation with Sarah White, August 28, 2014.

5. Conversation with Allen Blue, June 16, 2014.

6. Brian Chesky, "Belong Anywhere, *Airbnb Blog*, July 16, 2014, accessed August 28, 2014, http://blog.airbnb.com/belong-anywhere/.

7. Austin Carr, "What Hotel Operators Really Think of Airbnb," *Fast Company*, March 20, 2014, http://www.fastcompany.com.

INDEX

ABOUT THE AUTHOR

Robbie Kellman Baxter is the founder of Peninsula Strategies LLC, a consulting firm based in Menlo Park, CA, that helps companies excel in the Membership Economy. Her clients have included large organizations like Netflix, SurveyMonkey, and Yahoo!, as well as smaller venture-backed start-ups. Over the course of her career, Robbie has worked in or consulted with clients in more than 20 industries.

Before starting Peninsula Strategies in 2001, Robbie served as a New York City Urban Fellow, a consultant at Booz Allen & Hamilton, and a Silicon Valley product marketer. As a public speaker, Robbie has presented to thousands of people in corporations, associations, and universities.

Robbie has been quoted in or written articles for major media outlets, including *CNN*, *Consumer Reports*, *The New York Times*, and the *Wall Street Journal*. She has an AB from Harvard College and an MBA from the Stanford Graduate School of Business. Robbie's website is www.peninsulastrategies.com. She can be reached at rbaxter@peninsula-strategies.com.